The Play of Charles Dickens' Oliver Twist

Adapted by Nigel Bryant

Introduction and activities
by Angela Barrs

Series Editor: Lawrence Till

Heinemann Educational Publishers
Halley Court, Jordan Hill, Oxford OX2 8EJ
Part of Harcourt Education

Heinemann is the registered trademark of Harcourt Educational Limited

First published in Heinemann Floodlights 1983

First published in the *Heinemann Plays* series 1995

17

A catalogue record for this book is available from the British Library on request.

10-digit ISBN: 0 435233 13 0
13-digit ISBN: 978 0 435233 13 6

Cover design by Keith Pointing

Original design by Jeffrey White Creative Associates

Typeset by TechType, Abingdon, Oxon

Printed in the UK by Clays Ltd, St Ives plc

Acknowledgements
We would like to thank Time Out Magazine Ltd and The Royal Shakespeare
Company for permission to reproduce copyright material.

CONTENTS

INTRODUCTION

Charles Dickens and his Work (born 1812, died 1870)

Charles Dickens is considered by many people to be one of the greatest English novelists. His own childhood had much unhappiness in it: his father was imprisoned for debt and Charles was taken out of school and sent to work in a boot-polish factory when he was only 12. Dickens shows something of this nightmarish experience in *David Copperfield*, where the young David pastes labels onto bottles in an evil, rat-infested warehouse looking onto the River Thames. The scene drew on Dickens' own experience of child labour. As a writer, he was eager to make readers sympathize with his child characters who, like David Copperfield, were often orphaned, poor and isolated.

When Dickens wrote, he wanted not just to entertain his readers, many of whom had plenty of leisure and money to spend on reading novels; he also wanted to make them aware of social problems such as poverty and child labour. He believed that his readers could help improve society if they agreed with the moral viewpoints shown in his novels. Dickens created vivid characters, among them some dreadful adults, and made them look ridiculous or horrifying. Consider Scrooge from the short story *A Christmas Carol*. Even if you have not read the story, you will probably know about Scrooge, from a film or stage production, or simply because people today still use the name 'Scrooge' for a mean, miserable person. He is a cruel miser who hates people enjoying themselves, and part of the fun in reading (or watching) how Scrooge changes, comes from seeing him ridiculed. Scrooge becomes a good employer overnight, paying Bob Cratchit a decent wage so that he can provide a comfortable and healthy life for Tiny Tim and the rest of his family.

Dickens was also concerned about education, possibly because his own schooling had been cut short, which he greatly regretted. In *Nicholas Nickleby*, published in 1845, he created Dotheboys Hall, where children were sent as boarders and then conveniently forgotten. Schools like this existed in Yorkshire: 'places where children who were a nuisance or embarrassment to their parents or guardians could be sent and kept out of the way all year long...for a very modest cost.'[1]

Such schools made money out of their pupils by half-starving them and putting them in the charge of cruel and ignorant 'teachers', like Mr Wackford Squeers. Dickens wrote in his diary: '...the schoolmaster we saw today is the man in whose school several boys went blind sometime since from gross neglect.'[2]

After *Nicholas Nickleby* was published, schools such as Dotheboys Hall were obliged to improve, probably as a direct effect of Dickens' novel on the public conscience.

Oliver Twist and the Poor Law

Dickens began work on *Oliver Twist* in 1837 and finished it the following year. He felt particularly strongly about another way in which children were ill-treated. Desperately poor people, including the old, orphans and the sick, were often given money by the parish in which they lived. But some parishes did little to help and local residents resented contributing towards the growing number of poor people. In 1834, a Poor Law was brought in:

It grouped the parishes together in unions, which were ordered to build and run their own workhouses and save money by helping only those who went to live in them...

Life inside most workhouses was rarely as harsh as *The Times* and novels like *Oliver Twist* made out. Usually the paupers were fed adequately, but they were treated little better than criminals and made to feel so inferior that everyone avoided the workhouse until they were really destitute. Dread of the workhouse persisted in the later nineteenth century after their conditions improved. By then fewer than one per cent of the population was to be found inside a workhouse at any one moment (while over twice as many received relief), but about a quarter of the adults in Britain died in a workhouse or hospital run by the Poor Law.[3]

The law lasted until 1948!

Dickens felt that this law worsened the plight of many poor people and, in *Oliver Twist*, showed several ways in which this could happen. Oliver's mother is destitute and rejected by her family. She gives birth in the workhouse maternity room where she and her baby are despised because she is not married. Unmarried mothers had little support for themselves or their children. Oliver is sent to a 'baby farm' at another workhouse where the woman in charge takes the allowance for her own use and neglects the children so that, as Dickens writes in his novel, '...in eight and a half cases out of ten, either (the baby) sickened from want and cold, or fell into the fire from neglect, or got half smothered by accident; in any one of which cases, the miserable little being was usually summoned into another world, and there gathered to the fathers it had never known in this.'[4]

Dickens believed that young people brought up in such an uncaring way would be likely to turn to crime for a living, as do the Artful Dodger and Charley Bates in *Oliver Twist*. He felt too that workhouses had a negative effect on couples and families. He writes in *Oliver Twist* that workhouse administrators 'undertook to divorce poor married people, ...and instead of compelling a man to support his family, as they had theretofore done, took his family away from him, and made him a bachelor!'[5]

Charles Dickens and the Theatre

Dickens enjoyed reading his novels aloud to audiences and toured in this country and abroad. One of the last times he did so was to give a dramatic reading of the scene from *Oliver Twist* in which Bill Sikes murders Nancy. Apparently, he gave such a lively and exhausting performance that he hastened his own death. Many of the scenes in the novel are extremely dramatic and this is why it has been staged and filmed so many times. Just as Scrooge has become part of our culture, so have the famous scenes where Oliver asks for more and the young thieves play at pickpocketing in Fagin's den.

While Dickens was alive, many stage versions of his novels were made. From five hundred pages or more, a novel would be reduced in length for a short stage production. Nigel Bryant has had to shorten the story too, but has selected his scenes carefully, sometimes putting them in a different order from the novel, to keep the storyline clear. Although he has merged some characters together, he has kept all the characters readers remember best: Mr Bumble, the Artful Dodger, Fagin, Bill Sikes and Nancy. In the 'Explorations' section of this book, you can look closely at part of the play to see how it has been adapted from the novel. Most importantly, in order to keep the flavour of the original novel, Nigel Bryant has kept the language in which those characters speak. Through them, you can enjoy the drama of *Oliver Twist.*

Footnotes
1. Programme from Royal Shakespeare Company's production of *The Life and Adventures of Nicholas Nickelby* first performed at Royal Shakespeare Theatre, Stratford, 13 December 1985, Page 4.
2. As above.
3. *Britain Transformed: the development of British society since the mid-eighteenth century*, V.T.J. Arkell, Penguin Education, 1973, Page 113.
4. *Oliver Twist*, Charles Dickens, New Windmill Classics 1993, Page 5.
5. Page 12. Ibid.

A Note on Staging

This dramatization of *Oliver Twist* can be performed on almost any kind of stage, but the Victoria Theatre, Stoke-on-Trent, for which it was written, is a theatre in the round, a rectangular acting area surrounded by banked seating on all four sides. There are three direct entrances to the stage – two in the corners of one end of the rectangle and one in the middle of the other end – and three stairways through the audience which can also be used as acting entrances. Theatre in the round, with its intimacy and simplicity, lends itself excellently to all kinds of drama, and in particular has enormous potential for narrative plays like *Oliver Twist*. The six entrances of the Victoria Theatre at Stoke allow for rapid and varied flow from scene to scene; and above all, the great beauty of theatre in the round is that it demands the imaginative participation of the audience to fill out a setting. It is obviously impossible, with the audience on all four sides, to erect backdrops or to have literal sets with walls and doors and windows. Instead the design must simply *suggest* the setting of a scene and leave the audience to fill it out in their own minds. This is not only necessary; it is also very exciting. And it puts the emphasis of performance where it should be – on the play and on the players; it is the characters of *Oliver Twist* who make the atmosphere and set their own scenes, not lumps of set and furniture.

For a production of this version of *Oliver Twist*, whether played in the round or on a conventional stage, it is essential to have settings as simple and as minimal as possible. The scenes are often very short and scene changes need to be achieved at speed. Often, as well, two or more settings are on stage simultaneously. Consequently, in the Stoke production we used just a filthy old stove, two stools and a clothes-line of handkerchiefs to suggest Fagin's den; a bench and a table with a lectern-top upon it to suggest the police office; the same table with a shelf of books on top to suggest the bookstall of Scene 10; an old bed, the same two stools as before and a (slightly) different table for Sikes's house; two chairs and one of those small revolving bookstands with shelves on all four sides to suggest Mr Brownlow's; and nothing at all for Scenes 4, 5, 7, 14, 18 and many more. I think a complete inventory of our production's furniture would contain just: two benches, two stools, four tables, two chairs, the revolving bookstand, Sikes's bed, Fagin's stove and a dirty wooden pallet (for the workhouse room of Scenes 1 and 23). Not bad for an epic! By using the same items in different combinations and on different parts of the stage, utterly distinct places are conjured up in the audience's imagination. And often it is enough for an actor to appear in a police officer's uniform with a ledger in his hand to tell you that you are back in the office (Scene 14), or for another to appear in a doorman's gear to tell you that you are outside a hotel (Scene 31) – and in any case, as in the latter instance, the script time and again explicitly says where a scene is taking place. It is an exciting challenge for director and designer to work out what item or items will most richly and economically evoke a setting; then leave the cast and the audience to do the rest.

As an additional solution to practical problems posed by this adaptation of *Oliver Twist*, we included in the design of the Stoke production just one element of permanent set. It was a platform of slatted wood about two-and-a-half feet high, with a short flight of steps at each end; in one side of it was a pair of cupboard doors, so that Oliver could be piled through them and shut up beneath the platform when he is locked in the cellar by Mrs Sowerberry and Charlotte (Scene 6); and on top of the platform were a large trapdoor, through which Monks could drop the locket (Scene 29), and a very small trapdoor, which Toby Crackit could prise open to let Oliver climb through from underneath the platform during the burglary (Scene 24).

There are very few difficult *props* required, although it is essential to have a convincing dummy for the hanging of Bill Sikes (Scene 33) and a well-made fake new-born baby for Oliver's birth (Scene 1). There is no need for complex *lighting* effects either: lighting needs to be just sophisticated enough to define distinct areas of the stage, especially in the scenes with two or more simultaneous settings. It is important that the *costume* should emphasize the huge difference between the social classes of people in the play. In Scenes 13–20 (and elsewhere), when the London underworld of Sikes and Co. and the upper class world of Brownlow and Grimwig are on the acting area together – albeit in different settings on opposite sides of the stage – the contrast in costume can be very expressive; it can likewise add a great deal to the meeting between Rose and Nancy in Scene 31. It is important, too, to have incidental *music*, just in short bursts and phrases, to cover scene-changes and hectic bits of action like the fight in Scene 6 and the chase in Scene 10: it will sew the production together and sustain the play's momentum. For the Stoke production Jeff Parton composed six or seven tunes for solo 'cello, and recorded different verses and phrases in different ways for the various music cues.

At Stoke, as can be seen from the cast list, we performed the play with 8 men and 3 women. This is almost certainly the minimum possible; the maximum possible can be judged by counting the number of characters our cast played. Please note that, if following our doubling of Grimwig and Monks, the Alternative Scene 27 printed at the end of the playscript will need to be used.

I hope the notes above are useful; but they are intended only as *suggestions* for production. I'm sure there will be many other ways than ours of performing *Oliver Twist*.

Nigel Bryant

List of Characters

Surgeon
Old Sally
Oliver's Mother
Mrs Mann
Mr Bumble
Oliver Twist
2 Gentlemen Board Members
1 Lady Board Member
3 Workhouse Boys
Workhouse Master
Woman Server
Mr Sowerberry
Man Pauper
Woman Pauper
Dead Girl Pauper
Mrs Sowerberry
Charlotte
Noah Claypole
Artful Dodger
Woman in street
Charley Bates
Fagin
Mr Brownlow

Pieman
Policeman
2 Women in street
Police Officer
Fang
Bookseller
Bill Sikes
Nancy
Doctor
Mrs Bedwin
Mr Grimwig
Potato-seller
Old Woman
Young Surgeon
Servant Toby Crackit
Rose Grimwig
Monks
Doorman
3 Pursuers
Jailer
2 Workmen

For doubling of parts see Cast List for First Performance.

Cast List for First Performance

Oliver Twist by Nigel Bryant was first performed on 16 June 1982 at the Victoria Theatre, Stoke-on-Trent, with the following cast:

Brian Hickey	Surgeon (*Scene 1*)
	Workhouse Master (*Scene 3*)
	Noah Claypole
	Policeman (*Scenes 10 & 11*)
	Bill Sikes
Steven Granville	Oliver Twist
Kevin Burke	Mr Bumble
	Man (*Scene 8*)
	Police Officer (*Scenes 11 & 14*)
	Potato-seller (*Scene 18*)
	Servant (*Scene 24*)
	1st Pursuer (*Scene 33*)
	Workman (*Scene 34*)
David Plimmer	3rd Boy (*Scenes 2 & 3*)
	Charley Bates
	Doorman (*Scene 31*)
	Workman (*Scene 34*)
David Bowen	2nd Boy (*Scenes 2 & 3*)
	Man Pauper (*Scene 5*)
	2nd Man (*Scene 8*)
	Mr Brownlow
	Toby Crackit
Jim Wiggins	1st Gentleman Board Member (*Scene 3*)
	Fagin
Colum Convey	2nd Gentleman Board Member (*Scene 3*)
	Artful Dodger
Michael Lumsden	1st Boy (*Scene 3*)
	Mr Sowerberry
	Pieman (*Scene 10*)
	Fang
	Doctor (*Scene 13*)
	Mr Grimwig
	Young Surgeon (*Scene 23*)

	Mr Monks
	Policeman (*Scene 33*)
	Jailer (*Scene 34*)
Patricia England	Mrs Mann
	Woman Pauper (*Scene 5*)
	Bookseller (*Scene 11*)
	Woman (*Scene 18*)
	2nd Pursuer (*Scene 33*)
Roberta Kerr	Old Sally
	Woman Server (*Scene 3*)
	Dead Girl Pauper (*Scene 5*)
	Charlotte
	Woman (*Scene 10*)
	Nancy
Sarah Neville	Mother (*Scene 1*)
	Lady Board Member (*Scene 3*)
	Mrs Sowerberry
	Woman (*Scene 8*)
	2nd Woman (*Scene 10*)
	Mrs Bedwin
	Old Woman (*Scenes 21 & 23*)
	Rose Grimwig
	3rd Pursuer (*Scene 33*)

Director	Nigel Bryant
Designer	Leonard Birchenall
Music	Jeff Parton

Oliver Twist

Charles Dickens

PART ONE

Scene One

Darkness and stormy music. Suddenly the lights rise on the maternity room of a workhouse. In a filthy bed a young woman is giving birth, attended by a Surgeon and a drunken woman called Old Sally. Above the music and the Mother's cries of agony come shouts of:

Surgeon   Push! Push! It's nearly there!

Old Sally   It's coming! It's coming!

Surgeon   Come on! Push!

Old Sally   That's it, dear!

Surgeon   Fetch another blanket!

Old Sally   Cor!

Surgeon   Hurry up!

Old Sally staggers over to a table.

Old Sally   Blanket. Blanket.

Surgeon   You're half pickled in drink.

Old Sally   Oh, there's your blanket!

Mother   AAAHHH!

Surgeon   It's there. It's a boy.

Old Sally shouts to the mother.

Old Sally   Oh, it's a boy!

The Surgeon holds the baby upsidedown and slaps it.

Surgeon   Cry. Cry!

Old Sally   He doesn't want to breathe!

Surgeon   Come on. Come on.

Old Sally   Oh, he sneezed!

Surgeon   Cry!

A loud wail comes from the baby.

Old Sally	That was a good 'un!
	The Surgeon hands the baby to Old Sally.
	Cor, he's tiny.
Mother	Let me see the child before I die.
	The Surgeon washes his hands in a dirty, chipped bowl.
Surgeon	Oh, you mustn't talk about dying yet.
	He sits down and lights a pipe.
Old Sally	Lor, bless her dear heart, no! When she's lived as long as I have, and had thirteen childer of her own, and all of 'em dead except two, she'll know better than to take on like that, bless her heart. Think what it is to be a mother, there's a dear lamb, do!
Mother	Let me see him!
	Old Sally passes the baby to the mother, who kisses him, gazes wildly round, shudders, then dies. The Surgeon makes a brief attempt to revive her.
Surgeon	It's all over, Sally.
Old Sally	Ah, poor dear, so it is.
Surgeon	You needn't bother sending for me if the child cries, nurse. It's very likely it *will* be troublesome. Give it a little gruel if it is. She was a good-looking girl – where did she come from?
Old Sally	She was brought to this 'ere workhouse late last night. She was found lying in the street. She had walked some distance, for her shoes were worn to pieces; but where she came from, or where she was going to, nobody knows.
Surgeon	The old story – no wedding ring, I see. Ah, well! Good night, Sally.
Old Sally	Oh, good night, sir.
	As soon as the Surgeon is gone, Old Sally scuttles up to the dead mother, lifts up her head, and takes a locket from around her neck.

Old Sally	There's a thing! There's a thing!

She dangles the locket in front of her eyes, smiling. Music. The lights fade to black.

Scene Two

The lights rise on Oliver Twist scrubbing the floor of Mrs Mann's parlour at the junior workhouse. As soon as the music ends there are cries from offstage, and two Workhouse Boys rush on, pursued by Mrs Mann wielding a long cane.

Mrs Mann How dare you! Don't come to me with your everlasting tales of hunger! It'll be the coal-cellar next time, you ungrateful wretches, the coal-cellar! And you're just as bad, Oliver, you've been nothing but trouble since the moment you was born!

Loud knocking at the door. Bumble shouts from outside.

Bumble Mrs Mann!

Mrs Mann Goodness gracious! Is that you, Mr Bumble, sir? Take Oliver, you two brats, and wash 'im directly! My heart alive, Mr Bumble, how glad I am to see you, sure-ly! Don't dither, God's my life. It's the beadle!

Bumble shouts again from outside.

Bumble Mrs Mann!

Mrs Mann Coming, Mr Bumble, sir! I'd locked it on account of the infants, sir.

Bumble enters.

Bumble Do you think it proper conduct, Mrs Mann, to keep a parish officer a-waiting at your gate when he comes upon parish business concerning the parish orphans? Lead the way in, Mrs Mann, for I have something to say.

Mrs Mann Will you take a little drop of something, Mr Bumble?

Bumble Not a drop. Not a drop.

Mrs Mann	Just a little drop, with a little cold water and a lump of sugar?
	Bumble coughs.
Mrs Mann	Now, just a little drop.
Bumble	What is it?
Mrs Mann	It's what I'm obliged to keep a little of in the house to give the infants when they ain't well. It's gin. I'll not deceive you, Mr Bumble. It's gin.
Bumble	You give the infants gin, Mrs Mann?
Mrs Mann	Ah, bless 'em, that I do, dear as it is. I couldn't see 'em suffer, sir.
Bumble	You are a humane woman, Mrs Mann. I shall mention it to the board, Mrs Mann. You feel as a mother, Mrs Mann. I drink your health.
	He drinks.
	And now about business. The child as was baptized Oliver Twist is twelve years old today.
Mrs Mann	Bless him!
Bumble	And notwithstanding an offered reward of ten pound, afterward increased to twenty pound – notwithstanding the most supernatural exertions on the part of this parish, we have never been able to discover who is his father or what was his mother's name or condition.
Mrs Mann	How comes he to have any name at all, then?
Bumble	I invented it.
Mrs Mann	You, Mr Bumble!
Bumble	I, Mrs Mann. We name our orphans in alphabetical order. The last was a S. Swubble, I named him. This was a T. Twist, I named him. The next one as comes will be Unwin. The next Vilkins. I have got names ready made to the end of the alphabet, and all the way through it again when we come to Z.
Mrs Mann	Why, you're quite a literary character, sir!
Bumble	Well, well – perhaps I may be – perhaps I may be, Mrs Mann. Oliver being now too old to remain here

in the junior workhouse, the board have determined to have him back in the main house, for he is old enough now to be set to work, and I have come to take him there. So let me have him at once!

Mrs Mann Directly, sir! Oliver, hurry up!

Enter Oliver.

Make a bow to the gentleman, Oliver.

Oliver bows.

Bumble Will you come along with me, Oliver?

Oliver is about to agree immediately, but sees Mrs Mann, behind Bumble, shaking her fist in warning.

Oliver Will *she* go with me, sir?

Bumble No, she can't. But she'll come and see you sometimes.

Mrs Mann So there now, my dear little Oliver, no need to cry. Let me hug my little Oliver just once more.

Bumble There, there, Mrs Mann, no need to upset yourself. Give him a slice of bread and butter and he'll be happy. Got no affection in 'em but for what provides for their insatiable stomachs. No gratitude, Mrs Mann. No gratitude at all. Come here, Twist. I'm taking you before the board.

Scene Three

A short phrase of music as Bumble grabs Oliver and turns him round, and the lights rise on another part of the stage where we see Two Gentlemen Board Members and a Lady Board Member sitting behind a long table in the board room of the workhouse. In front of them are three silver plates covered with silver lids. The 1st Gentleman addresses Oliver, from a high chair.

1st Gentleman What's your name, boy?

Oliver does not reply immediately, so Bumble taps him on the head with his cane.

Bumble Answer, boy, and bow to the board.

Oliver The board, sir? Which board?

Bumble The board, boy! This lady and these here gentlemen!

1st Gentleman Well? What's your name?

Oliver Oliver Twist, sir.

1st Gentleman Listen to me, Twist. You know you're an orphan, I suppose?

Oliver What's that, sir?

2nd Gentleman The boy's a fool. I thought he was.

1st Gentleman Hush! You know you've got no father or mother, and that you were brought up by the parish, don't you?

Oliver cries.

Oliver Yes, sir.

2nd Gentleman What are you crying for? What *can* the boy be crying for?

Lady I hope you say your prayers every night, and pray for the people who feed you and take care of you, like a Christian?

Oliver Yes, ma'am.

1st Gentleman Well! You've come here to be educated and taught a useful trade.

2nd Gentleman So you'll begin to pick oakum at six o'clock in the morning.

The Board Members remove the lids over their plates to reveal three sumptuous meals.

What are you staring at, boy?

No reply: Oliver is speechless.

Lady The boy's a half-wit.

2nd Gentleman A waste of the parish's resources. It is a tragic irony that the wrong ones always live.

1st Gentleman Take him away, beadle. The sight of him depresses me.

Bumble You'll be just in time for supper, Twist. You don't deserve it, but some of us is just born lucky.

A short phrase of music. While the board continue their meal the lights dim on them, and rise on another part of the stage where a group of Workhouse Boys are picking oakum at a long table.

This is Twist, boys, Oliver Twist. You'll have to help with his education. Show him how to pick the rope, show him where to sit for his supper, and make sure he minds his manners.

Exit Bumble.

Oliver Hello.

1st Boy We're not supposed to talk at work-times.

Oliver Oh.

2nd Boy Not supposed to talk at meal-times.

3rd Boy Not supposed to *eat* at meal-times.

1st Boy Not supposed to live by the looks of it – not for long. My father kept a pie-shop: I'm not used to it: how can you live on three bowls of gruel a day?

2nd Boy Hush!

1st Boy An onion twice a week, and half a roll on Sundays. Don't go to the privy, Twist. There's so little going in, you daren't let nothing out. I tell you, if I don't have another basin of gruel a day, I'll wake up in the night and eat the lad as is lying next to me. You don't believe me, eh?

2nd Boy Hush!

1st Boy Never mind hush. We've got to have more.

3rd Boy You going to ask?

1st Boy I've had the brainwave: you do the asking.

3rd Boy No fear!

1st Boy You, Dick?

2nd Boy	Not me.
1st Boy	Twist, then, if you're all too scared.
3rd Boy	You're not, I suppose? Oh, no!
1st Boy	Twist's going.
2nd Boy	You can't pick on him the minute he arrives. None of us is going. You know we're not.
1st Boy	All right. We'll draw lots.
2nd Boy	What?
1st Boy	We'll draw lots. Everyone an equal chance. Here you are.
3rd Boy	Not me.
1st Boy	Lord love us. What do *you* say, Twist?
	No reply.
2nd Boy	It's the only way. Come on.
3rd Boy	God help me.
1st Boy	Quick.
	They draw lots. Oliver picks the short straw.
3rd Boy	Oliver!
1st Boy	Born lucky, Oliver! You ask. They're coming!
	The Master and a Woman Server enter. The Boys line up, receive a bowl from the Server, and the Master slops a portion of gruel into each one from a pot. The Boys sit at the table.
Woman Server	For what.
Boys	We are about to receive, may the Lord make us truly thankful. Amen.
	They eat. Then all wait for Oliver to go and ask. Oliver finally takes his bowl up to the Master.
Oliver	Please, sir, I want some more.
	Dumbstruck silence.
Master	What?

Oliver   Please, sir, I want some more.

Music. The Master takes a swing at him with the ladle, grabs him and screams for Mr Bumble. The lights shift back to the boardroom as Bumble and the Master haul Oliver before the Board.

Bumble   Mr Limbkins, I beg your pardon, sir! Oliver Twist has asked for more!

1st Gentleman For more! Compose yourself, Bumble, and answer me distinctly. Do I understand that he asked for more, after he had eaten the supper allotted by the dietary?

Bumble   He did, sir.

2nd Gentleman That boy will be hung. I know that boy will be hung.

Lady   The first day here, the first hour here, and he asks for more!

1st Gentleman Confine him instantly, beadle, and post a bill on the gate offering a reward of one pound –

2nd Gentleman Five pounds!

1st Gentleman Five pounds to anyone who will take him off the hands of the parish.

2nd Gentleman I never was more convinced of anything in my life, than I am that that boy will come to be hung.

Music. Lights fade.

Scene Four

Lights rise on Mr Bumble, outside the workhouse, nailing the bill to a post. Sowerberry, the undertaker, enters.

Sowerberry   Good morning, Mr Bumble.

Bumble   Mr Sowerberry, good morning to you.

Sowerberry   I have finished the coffins for the two workhouse women who died last night, Mr Bumble.

Bumble   You'll make your fortune, sir. I should have been an undertaker myself.

He hands him some money.

What an ingenious snuffbox that is, sir, shaped like a coffin! I say you'll make your fortune, sir.

Sowerberry   Think so, Mr Bumble? The prices you pay at the workhouse are very small.

Bumble   So are the coffins.

Sowerberry   Oh, true, Mr Bumble, true! Since you brought in the new system of feeding the poor, the coffins are something narrower and shallower than they used to be. But we must have some profit, Mr Bumble. Well-seasoned timber is an expensive article, sir; and all the iron handles come by canal from Birmingham.

Bumble   Well, every trade has its drawbacks. You don't know anyone as wants a boy, do you? An apprentice, who is at present a deadweight, a millstone as you might say round the parish's throat? Generous terms, Mr Sowerberry, generous terms!

Bumble taps the bill.

Sowerberry   Five pounds! Gadso!

Bumble   A fair offer, eh? Have him on approval, sir, on approval.

Sowerberry   You know, Mr Bumble, I pay a good deal in rates for the upkeep of the poor.

Bumble   So?

Sowerberry   Well, I was thinking that if I pay so much towards 'em, I've a right to get as much out of 'em as I can. I'll take the boy, Mr Bumble, indeed I will.

Bumble   Let me shake you by the hand, sir. One five pound note, sir, and the boy shall be delivered to you within the hour! There he is now – Oliver!

Sowerberry   Ah, well, let me take him at once. I've a dead body to collect in the village – I could do with an extra pair of hands.

Oliver enters, staggering under the weight of a huge pile of old rope.

This is the boy, is it? Dear me, he's very small.

Bumble Yes, he is rather small. He is small, there's no denying it. But he'll grow, Mr Sowerberry, he'll grow.

Sowerberry I dare say he will, on our food and our drink. I'm a fool! There's no saving in parish children. They cost more to keep than they're worth. Howsoever, follow me, er –

Bumble Twist, Oliver Twist.

Sowerberry Oliver Twist. We've work to do.

Bumble impatiently snatches the rope from the bewildered Oliver.

Bumble Go on, Twist! You're going with the gentleman! And I'm glad to see the back of you!

Music. Lights fade.

Scene Five

Lights up on a pauper's hovel. Paupers in rags are sitting around the body of a girl wrapped in an old blanket. Sowerberry appears outside the hovel with Oliver.

Sowerberry No knocker or bell. Hello! Mr Sowerberry. Undertaker. And Oliver Twist.

Man Pauper Nobody shall go near her! Keep back! Damn you, keep back, if you've a life to lose!

Sowerberry Nonsense, my good man, nonsense!

Man Pauper I tell you I won't have her put into the ground. She couldn't rest there. The worms would worry her – not eat her – she's so worn away.

Sowerberry kneels down and starts measuring the body.

Ah! Kneel down, kneel down – kneel round her, every one of you, and mark my words. I say she was starved to death. I never knew how bad she was till the fever came upon her; and then her bones were starting through the skin. There was neither fire nor candle; she died in the dark – in the dark! She couldn't even see her children's faces, though we heard her gasping out their names. I had no work, so I went and begged for her in the streets – and they arrested me for begging and sent me to prison! When I came back she was dying; and all the blood in my heart has dried up, for they killed her! They starved her to death! I swear it before the God that saw it! They starved her!

He screams and rolls in a fit on the floor. An Old Woman Pauper loosens his cravat and says:

Woman Pauper She was my daughter. Lord, lord! Well it is a strange thing that I who gave birth to her, and was a woman then, should be alive and merry now, and she lying there so cold and stiff. To think of it – it's as good as a play – as good as a play!

Sowerberry We'd best take the body now, Oliver. We'll never get it from these Bedlam-cases if we come back for it tomorrow. Give me a hand.

Man Pauper Where are they taking her? Leave her be! Leave her be!

Woman Pauper Lord, lord!

Sowerberry Quickly, Oliver! Get off me, man!

Man Pauper Oh, God! They killed her! They killed her!

Sowerberry Out now, Oliver, while we can!

Sowerberry and Oliver lug the body out and away. The Woman Pauper shouts after them.

Woman Pauper Will she be buried tomorrow? Send me a cloak: a good warm one, for it's bitter cold. And some bread – just a loaf of bread and a cup of water. Shall we have some bread, dear?

Music. Lights fade.

Scene Six

*Lights up on Sowerberry and Oliver entering
Sowerberry's shop.*

Sowerberry Well, then, Oliver, how did you like your first day as
an apprentice undertaker?

Oliver Pretty well, thank you, sir. Not very much, sir.

Sowerberry Ah, you'll get used to it in time, Oliver. Nothing when
you *are* used to it, my boy. And nothing's what you
earn from these parish funerals for these crazy-headed
paupers. Still it's a nice sickly season at present. In
commercial phrase, Oliver, coffins are looking up.

Mrs Sowerberry enters.

Mrs Sowerberry This is the boy, is it? He's very small.

Sowerberry Yes, dear, he is rather small. But he'll grow.

He goes.

Mrs Sowerberry Sit over there, you little bag o' bones.

Charlotte enters.

Here, Charlotte, give this boy some of the cold bits
that were put by for the dog. He hasn't come home
since the morning, so he can go without 'em. I dare
say the boy ain't too dainty to eat 'em – are you, boy?

Oliver No, ma'am.

Mrs Sowerberry And when you've finished, your bed's under the
counter. You don't mind sleeping among the coffins, do
you? It's bad luck if you do, for you can't sleep nowhere
else. See to 'im, Charlotte. I can't stay up all night.

She goes.

Charlotte There y'are. It's a right dog's dinner!

She laughs.

From the workhouse, are you?

Oliver wolfs down the food.

Oliver Yes, ma'am.

Charlotte Oh, Lor, 'e calls *me* ma'am an' all! Oh, hello, Noah.

Noah Claypole enters.

Noah Claypole	Yer the new boy, are yer?
Oliver	Yes, sir.
Noah	Born and bred in the workhouse, I hear?
Oliver	Yes, sir.
Noah	How old are yer?
Oliver	Twelve, sir.
Noah	Then I'll wop yer when yer've finished, you just see if I don't, yer workhouse brat! I'm Mister Noah Claypole, and you're under me!
Charlotte	Come near the fire, Noah, I saved you a nice bit of bacon from master's breakfast. Let the boy alone.
Noah	Let him alone? Everyone lets him alone, I should think. Bet his father and mother don't interfere with him too much! All his relations let him have his own way pretty well, eh, Charlotte?
	He laughs.
Charlotte	You queer soul!
Noah	Pretty is she, your mother?
Oliver	She's dead. Don't you say anything about her to me.
Noah	What did she die of, Work'us?
Oliver	Of a broken heart, some of the nurses told me. I think I know what it must be to die of that.
Noah	Tol de rol lol lol right fol lairy, Work'us. What's set you a-snivelling now?
Oliver	Not you – don't think it.
Noah	Oh, not me, eh?
Oliver	No, not you. There; that's enough. Don't say anything more to me about her. You'd better not.
Noah	Better not! Well! Better not! Work'us, don't be impudent. With a mother what died in the workhouse you've no right to be impudent. Bet she was a nice'un, eh, Charlotte, giving birth in the workhouse. We know what that sort's like. Oh Lor! Yer know, Work'us, it can't be helped now, and of course yer couldn't help it then, and I'm very sorry for it; and I'm sure we all are and pity yer very much.

But yer must know, Work'us, your mother was a regular right-down bad'un.

Oliver What did you say?

Noah A regular right-down bad'un, Work'us. And it's a great deal better that she died when she did, or else she'd have been hard-labouring in Bridewell Prison, or transported, or hung; which is more likely than either, isn't it?

Frenzied music as Oliver pounces on Noah and brings him crashing to the floor.

He'll murder me! Charlotte! Missis! The new boy's a-murdering me! Help! Help!! Oliver's gone mad! Charlotte!

Charlotte Oh, you little wretch! You little, ungrateful, murderous, horrid villain!

Mrs Sowerberry enters and grabs Oliver, who scratches at her face. A terrible fight, in which all three beat and pommel at Oliver, drag him into a cellar and lock him up. Then Mrs Sowerberry collapses into a chair. The music stops.

Mrs Sowerberry Oh, Charlotte. It's a mercy we haven't all been murdered in our beds.

Charlotte This'll teach master not to have any more of these dreadful creatures. They're born to be murderers and robbers from their very cradle. Poor Noah, he was all but killed, ma'am.

Mrs Sowerberry Poor fellow!

Oliver hammers on the cellar door.

What's to be done? He'll kick that door down in ten minutes!

Charlotte Send for the police-officers.

Noah Or the milingtary.

Mrs Sowerberry No, no. Run to Mr Bumble, Noah, and tell him to come here directly. Never mind your cap! Make haste! You can hold a knife to that black eye as you run along. It'll keep the swelling down.

Noah rushes out.

God's my life! And to think the dog's gone hungry for him!

Short burst of music as the lights dim on them and rise on the other side of the stage where Noah rushes into the workhouse yard to find Bumble.

Noah   Mr Bumble! Mr Bumble! Oh,.Mr Bumble, sir, Oliver, sir, Oliver has –

Bumble   What? What? Not run away? He hasn't run away, has he, Noah?

Noah   No, sir, not run away, sir, but he's turned vicious. He tried to murder me, sir; and then he tried to murder Charlotte, and then missis. Oh, the agony, sir!

The 2nd Gentleman enters.

2nd Gentleman   What's going on, Bumble? What's the matter with the youth?

Bumble   The poor boy has been nearly murdered – all but murdered, sir – by young Twist.

2nd Gentleman   I knew it! I felt a strange presentiment from the very first that that audacious young savage would come to be hung!

Bumble   He has likewise attempted, sir, to murder the female servant.

Noah   And the missis.

Bumble   And the master, too, I think you said, Noah?

2nd Gentleman   You're a very good boy. Here's a penny for you. Bumble, step up to Sowerberry's with your cane and don't spare him. Don't spare him, Bumble!

Bumble   I will not, sir!

Bumble and Noah go. The 2nd Gentleman calls after them.

2nd Gentleman   Tell Sowerberry not to spare him, either. They'll never do anything with him without stripes and bruises.

Short burst of music as the lights rise on Bumble and Noah returning to Sowerberry's shop.

Bumble   Oliver!

Oliver   Come, you let me out!

Bumble   Do you know this here voice, Oliver?

Oliver   Yes.

Bumble   Ain't you afraid of it, sir? Ain't you a-trembling while I speak, sir?

Oliver   No!

Mrs Sowerberr   Oh! Mr Bumble, he must be mad. No boy in half his senses could venture to speak so to you!

Bumble suddenly spots the bits of meat scattered during the fight.

Bumble   It's not madness, ma'am. It's meat.

Mrs Sowerberry   What?

Bumble   Meat, ma'am, meat. You've overfed him, ma'am. You've raised a artificial soul and spirit in him, ma'am, unbecoming a person of his condition, as the board, Mrs Sowerberry, who are practical philosophers, will tell you. What have paupers to do with soul and spirit? It's quite enough that we let 'em have live bodies. If you had kept him on gruel this would never have happened.

Mrs Sowerberry   Dear dear! This comes of being generous!

Bumble   Keep him in the cellar for a day or so, until he's starved down. Then keep him on gruel. He comes of a bad family. Excitable natures. Both the nurse and the surgeon said that that mother of his made her way here against difficulty and pain as would have killed any decent woman weeks before.

Oliver   Don't talk about her! Don't you talk about her!

Oliver kicks and hammers at the door.

Bumble   Leave him there to starve down, Mrs Sowerberry. And don't give him any more meat.

The lights dim as they all go, leaving Oliver hammering in the shadows. Suddenly the lock breaks and the cellar door flies open. Oliver emerges, listens nervously, wraps a piece of bread and butter in a handkerchief, and begins to creep out of the room. He knocks over a saucepan in the dark. Charlotte shouts from offstage.

Charlotte   Here! What was that noise?

Burst of music as Oliver runs for it and Charlotte and Mrs Sowerberry rush back in.

Charlotte   He's gone, missis, he's gone!

Mrs Sowerberry   Lord love us, he's a monster! We're better off without him!

Music. Lights fade.

Scene Seven

Dawn rises on Oliver, dirty and exhausted, sitting at the side of a road, eyes closed. The Artful Dodger enters, whistling the tune of 'Botany Bay'. He stops, studies Oliver, and sees him stir. He goes and sits beside him.

Dodger   Hullo, my covey! What's the row?

Oliver   I'm very hungry and tired. I've walked a long way. I've been walking these seven days.

Dodger   Walking for seven days! Oh, I see. Beak's order, eh?

Oliver looks puzzled.

Don't you know what a beak is, my flash companion?

Oliver   Yes. It's a bird's mouth.

Dodger   My eyes, how green! A beak's a magistrate. And when you walk by a beak's order it's not straightforerd, but always a-goin' up, and never a-comin' down again. Was you never on the mill?

Oliver	What mill?
Dodger	What mill! Why, *the* mill – the treadmill. My eyes, he ain't twigged yet! But come – you want grub, and you shall have it! What has he got in his pockets, I hear you ask.
	Dodger dips into his voluminous coat pockets.
	A bob's worth of ham and a four-penny bran, not to mention a bottleful of swipes! Have a lush of that!
	He produces ham, bread and a bottle of beer.
	Going to London?
Oliver	Yes.
Dodger	Got any lodgings?
Oliver	No.
Dodger	Money?
Oliver	No.
	Dodger whistles.
	Do you live in London?
Dodger	Yes, I do, when I'm at home. I suppose you want some place to sleep in tonight, don't you?
Oliver	I do indeed. I haven't slept under a roof since I left the country.
Dodger	Don't fret your eyelids on that score. I've got to be in London tonight; and I know a respectable old gentleman as lives there, wot'll give you lodgings for nothink, and never ask for the change – that is, if any gentelman he knows interduces you. And don't he know me? Oh, no! Not in the least! By no means! Certainly not! What's your name?
Oliver	Oliver Twist.
Dodger	My eyes! I suppose you want to know mine?
Oliver	Well – yes.
Dodger	Which one?
Oliver	Pardon?
Dodger	I, my covey, am John Dawkins, otherwise known as Jack, otherwise known to my more intimate associates as the Artful Dodger.

Oliver   Oh.

Dodger   Tell yer wot, Oliver: finish that off on the way. We'll have a good long stop before we get to London, so you can polish off the rest while it gets dark. I don't like London in the daytime, know wot I mean?

Music. Lights fade as Dodger leads Oliver away.

Scene Eight

Lights rise on a London backstreet, late at night. A Woman pushes a Man out of a public house doorway.

Woman   Leave him be! You leave him be!

1st Man   I'll mark him! I'll settle his score!

2nd Man   Leave him, Bet. It's him and me!

Woman   He's got a knife! Get back inside!

2nd Man   I'll have it off him.

Woman   You thick-skulled –

Dodger enters and sees this with Oliver.

Dodger   Not a happy band, Oliver. Definitely not a happy band. Watch yourself!

The fight flashes past them.

It's that sort as spoils the neighbourhood. Follow me.

Dodger and Oliver step up to a doorway. Dodger whistles.

Charley Bates   Now then!

Dodger   Plummy and slam!

Charley   Who's the other one?

Dodger   A new pal.

Charley   Where did he come from?

Dodger   *Green*land! Is Fagin upstairs?

Charley   Yes. Come on up.

Music. Lights fade on them and rise on another part

of the stage where Fagin is frying sausages on a rusty old stove. Dozens of silk handkerchiefs are hanging on a line. The Boys enter.

Dodger   I've got a new pal, Fagin. My friend Oliver Twist.

Fagin   Indeed, indeed.

He grins and bows to Oliver.

I hope I shall have the honour of your intimate acquaintance, Oliver.

Charley   Let me take your bundle, Oliver.

Dodger takes Oliver's cap.

I'll empty your pockets, too. Uncomfy when you lie down. Ow!

Fagin raps him with a toasting fork.

Fagin   We are very glad to see you, Oliver, very. Dodger, take off the sausages; and draw a tub near the fire for Oliver. Ah, you're a-staring at the pocket-handkerchiefs! Eh, my dear! There are a good many of 'em, ain't there? We've just looked 'em out, ready for the wash; that's all, Oliver; that's all.

He laughs.

But you look tired, my dear.

Oliver nods.

Yes, well. Here's some gin and water – hot, my dear, hot. Just you drink it down directly, Oliver.

Charley   Yeah, do that, Oliver: I needs the tumbler.

He laughs.

Oliver knocks back the gin and water and passes out on the spot. Fagin catches him and carries him gently to a pile of blankets on the floor.

Fagin   A fine young friend you've found here, Dodger.

Dodger   Yeah. And he's so very green!

Music. Lights fade.

Scene Nine

Lights up on the same room next morning. Dodger and Charley have gone out. Oliver is still asleep. Fagin is stirring something in a saucepan. He stops, and looks at Oliver.

Fagin   Oliver.

There is no reply.

Oliver.

Still no reply, so Fagin draws a small box from a hiding-place and sets it on the table. From it he draws a gold watch and chain.

Aha! Clever dogs! Clever dogs! Staunch to the last! Never split on old Fagin. And why should they? It wouldn't have loosened the hangman's knot. No, no, no! Fine fellows, fine fellows!

He draws out more treasures: rings, bracelets of a magnificent kind. Unbeknown to Fagin, Oliver wakes up and gazes at him.

What a fine thing capital punishment is! Dead men never repent; dead men never bring awkward stories to light. Five of 'em strung up in a row, and none left to turn lily-livered and split on old Fagin!

Fagin suddenly sees Oliver watching him, and slams the box shut in horror. He snatches up a bread-knife and starts furiously up.

What's that? What do you watch me for? Why are you awake? What have you seen? Speak out, boy! Quick – quick, for your life.

Oliver   I wasn't able to sleep any longer, sir. I'm very sorry if I've disturbed you, sir.

Fagin   You weren't awake an hour ago?

Oliver   No, no, indeed!

Fagin	Are you sure?
Oliver	Upon my word I was not, sir. I was not indeed, sir.

Fagin plays with the knife nonchalantly.

Fagin   Tush, tush, my dear. Of course I know that, my dear. I only tried to frighten you. You're a brave boy. You're a brave boy, Oliver! Did you see any of these pretty things, my dear?

Oliver   Yes, sir.

Fagin   Ah! They're mine – yes, they're mine, Oliver; my little property. All I have to live upon in my old age. Folks call me a miser, my dear; only a miser, that's all.

Oliver   May I get up now, sir?

Fagin   Certainly, my dear, certainly. There's a pitcher of water and a basin by the door, to wash in.

While Oliver goes to wash, Fagin conceals his box again. Just as he does so Charley Bates and the Dodger enter.

Dodger   Bon jooer!

Fagin   Well, I hope you've been at work this morning, my dears?

Dodger   Hard.

Charley   As nails.

Fagin   Good boys, good boys! What have *you* got, Dodger?

Dodger   A couple of wallets.

Fagin   Lined?

Dodger produces two wallets.

Dodger   Pretty well.

Fagin   Not so heavy as they might be, but very neat and nicely made. Ingenious workman, ain't he, Oliver?

Oliver   Very, indeed, sir.

Charley Bates laughs uproariously.

Fagin   And what have *you* got, Charley, my dear?

Charley   Wipes.

He produces four handkerchiefs.

Fagin   Well, they're very good ones, very. You haven't
             initialled them well though, Charley; so the initials
             shall be picked out with a needle, and we'll teach
             Oliver how to do it. Shall us, Oliver, eh?

Oliver   If you please, sir.

Fagin   You'd like to be able to make pocket-handkerchiefs
             as easy as Charley Bates, wouldn't you, my dear?

Oliver   Very much indeed, sir, if you'll teach me.

*Charley Bates nearly chokes himself laughing on his
coffee.*

Charley He's so jolly green!

Dodger smooths Oliver's hair over his eyes.

Dodger   He'll know better by and by.

Fagin   Did you go to the execution, Dodger?

Dodger   Yeah.

Fagin   Was there much of a crowd there?

Dodger   Quite a few, quite a few. Lapping it up, they was.

Oliver   How did you find time to make the handkerchiefs,
             then?

Charley Bates roars with laughter again.

Fagin   We've a little game to show you, Oliver. Haven't we,
             boys?

Charley I haven't finished me breakfast yet.

Fagin   Come along, come along. Time enough for that.
             Watch closely, Oliver.

Dodger   It's highly educational.

*Music. Fagin stuffs his coat pockets with a watch, a
wallet, handkerchiefs etc., and mimes an old
gentleman window-shopping. Dodger and Charley
act out pickpocketing: if Fagin feels their hands in
his pockets the game starts again. Oliver finds it great
fun.*

Fagin	There, Oliver. Good at the game, aren't they?
Oliver	Yes indeed, sir.
Dodger	Months of practice, mark you, Oliver.
Fagin	Make 'em your models, my dear. Make 'em your models. Do everything they bid you, and take their advice in all matters – especially the Dodger's, my dear.
Charley	Here!
Fagin	He'll be a great man himself, and will make you one, too, if you follow his example. Is my handkerchief hanging out of my pocket, my dear?
Oliver	Yes, sir.
Fagin	See if you can take it out without my feeling it, as you saw them do.
	Oliver does it perfectly.
	Is it gone?
Oliver	Here it is, sir.
Fagin	You're a clever boy, my dear! I never saw a sharper lad. Here's a shilling for you. If you go on in this way you'll be the greatest man of the time!
Dodger	Want to come out with us, Oliver? Get some instruction in our industry?
Oliver	May I, sir?
Fagin	You couldn't be in better hands, my dear. Take good care of him, Dodger. Give him the best of your tuition.
Charley	Here's yer cap. Come on. Time to pad the hoof.
Fagin	Don't give him too long a study – not the first time.
Dodger	Cheerio.
	Music. Lights fade.

Scene Ten

Lights rise on a busy street in Clerkenwell. Mr Brownlow is browsing at a bookstall. Dodger, Charley and Oliver enter. Dodger and Charley steal pies from a Pieman's tray while Oliver innocently buys a pie with his shilling. Dodger makes a sudden stop, finger on lips.

Oliver   What's the matter?

Dodger   Hush! You see that old cove at the bookstall?

Oliver   The old gentleman over the way? Yes, I see him.

Charley   A prime plant.

Charley and Dodger creep up and pick Mr Brownlow's pocket. Oliver watches in horror, suddenly understanding. Dodger and Charley run off. Mr Brownlow feels in his pocket, spins round, sees Oliver turn and run, and assumes the worst.

Mr Brownlow   Stop, thief! Stop, thief!

Pieman   Here! Stop, you little villain! Stop!

Music. All hell breaks loose. Tradesmen and Public pursue Oliver, as indeed do Dodger and Charley, until they see a good moment to slip away; while the Pieman is gone a Woman shovels his pies into her pram. Finally Oliver is felled by a mighty blow from the Pieman. A great crowd gathers round him.

Policeman   Stand aside!

1st Woman   Give him a little air!

The Pieman nurses an injured fist.

Pieman   Nonsense! He don't deserve it!

2nd Woman   Where's the gentleman?

1st Woman   Here he is, coming down the street.

Policeman   Make room there for the gentleman! Is this the boy, sir?

Brownlow	Yes. Yes, I am afraid it is.
Pieman	Afraid? That's a good 'un!
Brownlow	Poor fellow. He has hurt himself.
Pieman	I did that, sir! And preciously cut me knuckles against his mouth. I stopped him, sir!
Policeman	Come on, get up!
Oliver	It wasn't me indeed, sir! Indeed, indeed, it was two other boys! They're here somewhere.
Policeman	Oh, no, they ain't. Come on, get up!
Brownlow	Don't hurt him.
Policeman	Oh no, I won't hurt him. I know what you're up to, and it won't work. Will you stand up on your legs, you young devil?

Oliver staggers up and the Policeman instantly lugs him away. Brownlow rushes after him.

Brownlow	Don't hurt the boy, I say!
Pieman	Well swipe me! I bleed me bloomin' knuckles and do I get a reward? Do I ever? Don't hurt the thieving villain! Oh my life! We're getting soft! Soft! Here! Who's had me bloomin' pies?

Music. Lights fade.

Scene Eleven

Lights up on the Police Station. The Policeman hauls in Oliver, followed by Brownlow. They are met by a Police Officer with a bunch of keys.

Officer	What's the matter now?
Policeman	A young fogle-hunter.
Officer	Are you the party that's been robbed, sir?
Brownlow	Yes, I am. But I'm not sure that this boy actually took the handkerchief. I – I would rather not press the case.

Officer	Must go before the magistrate now, sir. His worship Mr Fang will be disengaged in half a minute.

Oliver is dumped on a bench and handcuffed. Brownlow gazes at him.

Brownlow	I'm sure the boy is innocent.
Policeman	Oh yes. Get 'em in the station, get 'em in the court, butter wouldn't melt in their mouths.
Brownlow	But there's something in that boy's face – God bless my soul – where have I seen something like that look before?
Policeman	Stained glass winders, sir. Little angels, the lot of 'em. Oh, here you are: here's the magistrate.

Mr Fang enters. Brownlow presents his card to him.

Brownlow	That is my name and address, sir.
Fang	Who are you?

Brownlow, surprised, points at his card. Fang throws it away.

Officer! Who is this fellow?

Brownlow	My name, sir, is Brownlow. Permit me to inquire the name of the magistrate who offers a gratuitous and unprovoked insult to a respectable person, under the protection of the bench.
Fang	Officer, what's this fellow charged with?
Policeman	He's not charged at all, your worship. He appears against this boy.
Fang	Appears against the boy, does he? Swear him.
Brownlow	Before I am sworn I must beg to say one word, and that is that I really never, without actual experience, could have believed –
Fang	Hold your tongue, sir!
Brownlow	I will not, sir!

Fang   Hold your tongue this instant or I'll have you turned out of this office! You're an insolent, impertinent fellow! How dare you bully a magistrate?

Brownlow   What!

Fang   I'll not hear another word from you, sir! Now, what's the charge against this boy?

Brownlow   I was standing at a bookstall –

Fang   Hold your tongue, sir! Policeman! What's the charge?

Policeman Pickpocketing, your worship. The hue and cry's set up in a court off Clerkenwell Green, a crowd pursues the boy and catches him. I search him, your worship, but I find nothing on his person, sir; and that's all I know about it.

Fang   Are there any witnesses to the offence?

Policeman None, your worship.

Fang   Then state your complaint against the boy, sir! If you stand there refusing to give evidence I'll punish you for disrespect to the bench!

Brownlow   I ran after the boy because I saw him running away, but I am not sure that he was the thief –

Fang   Ha!

Brownlow   He may be connected with thieves, but if he is he has been punished already. He has been hurt, sir, hurt – and I fear, I really fear he is very ill.

Fang   Oh yes! I dare say! Come, none of your tricks here, you young vagabond; they won't do. What's your name?

               Oliver tries to reply but can't: his head is spinning.

               What's your name, you hardened scoundrel? Officer, what's his name?

               The Officer bends over Oliver and realizes Oliver is beyond replying.

Officer   He says his name's Tom White, your worship.

Fang   Oh, he won't speak out, eh? Very well. Where does he live?

The Officer again pretends to hear Oliver.

Officer   Where he can, your worship.

Fang   Has he any parents?

Officer   He says they died in his infancy, your worship.

Oliver   Please may I have a draught of water?

Fang   Stuff and nonsense! Don't try to make a fool of me!

Officer   I think he really is ill, your worship.

Fang   I know better.

Brownlow   Take care of him, officer, he'll fall down!

Fang   Stand away, officer; let him, if he likes.

Oliver crashes to the floor.

There! I knew he was pretending! Let him lie there; he'll soon be tired of it.

Fang starts to go.

Policeman   Er – how do you propose to deal with the case, sir?

Fang   Summarily. He stands committed for three months – hard labour, of course. Clear the office.

Fang starts to go again.

A Bookseller bursts into the room.

Bookseller   Stop! Stop! Don't take him away! For Heaven's sake stop a moment!

Fang   What's this? Who is this? Turn this person out! Clear the office!

Bookseller   I *will* speak! I will not be turned out. I saw it all. I keep the bookstall. I will not be put down! Mr Fang, you must hear me. You must not refuse, sir!

Fang   Let's hear you, then. What have you got to say?

Bookseller   This. I saw three boys – two others and the prisoner here – loitering across the street while the gentleman was reading. The theft was committed by another boy – I saw it done. And I saw that this boy was perfectly amazed and stupefied by it.

Fang Why didn't you come here before?

Bookseller I hadn't a soul to mind the shop – everyone had joined in the hue and cry. I could get no-one until five minutes ago, and I've run here all the way.

Fang The prosecutor was reading, was he?

Bookseller Yes, sir, the very book he has in his hand.

Fang Oh, that book, eh? Is it paid for?

The Bookseller smiles.

Bookseller No, it is not.

Brownlow Dear me, I forgot all about it!

Fang A nice person to prefer charges against a poor boy! You have obtained that book under very suspicious circumstances: consider yourself lucky not to be prosecuted. Let this be a lesson to you, my man. The boy is discharged. Clear the office!

Brownlow Damn me! Damn me, I'll –

Fang Clear the office! Officers, do you hear? Clear the office!

Officer Come along, sir. You'd better do as he says.

Brownlow I'd never have believed it. Never.

Brownlow starts to go.

Policeman What are you going to do with the boy, sir?

Brownlow Oh, the poor fellow! I'm taking him home with me! Call a cab directly! Poor boy! Poor boy! There's no time to lose!

He starts to take Oliver out, but the Bookseller stops him.

Bookseller Er – The book costs one and six, sir.

Brownlow Oh. Bless me, yes. Bless me. Oh.

He hands the book back to the Bookseller and goes. The Bookseller is not pleased. Music. Lights fade.

Scene Twelve

Lights rise on Charley Bates and Dodger entering outside Fagin's den. Charley is laughing hysterically.

Charley   Oh, my eyes!

Dodger   What's up with you?

Charley   Ha! Ha! Ha!

Dodger   Hold your noise! Do you want to be grabbed, stupid?

Charley   I can't help it! I can't help it! To see him splitting away like that, cutting round the corners, knocking against the posts, and me with the old cove's wipe in me pocket, singin' out arter 'im – oh my eyes!

Dodger   Yeah, 'ighly comical. What's Fagin going to say?

Charley   What?

Dodger   Ah, what?

Charley   Why, what should he say? What should he say?

Dodger takes off his hat, scratches his head and whistles three times.

What do you mean?

Dodger   Toor rul lol loo, gammon and spinnage, the frog he wouldn't and high cockalorum.

Charley   What do you mean?

The lights shift across the stage, and Dodger and Charley move into Fagin's den.

Fagin   Why, how's this? Only two of 'em? Where's the third? You haven't got into trouble? Where's Oliver, you young hounds? Where's the boy? What's become of the boy?

Fagin seizes Dodger.

Speak out, damn you, or I'll throttle you!

Charley drops to his knees and moans in terror.
Will you speak?

Dodger   The traps have got him, and that's all about it!
Come, let go o'me, will you!

*Dodger breaks loose and threatens Fagin with the
toasting-fork.*

Fagin   Why, you –

*Dodger lunges at Fagin with the fork: Fagin steps back
and roars as he hurls a mug of ale at Dodger: suddenly
Bill Sikes enters, followed by Nancy.*

Sikes   What the blazes is in the wind now? Who pitched
that here at me? It's lucky it's the beer and not the
pot as hit me, or I'd have settled somebody. Oh! I
might have know'd as no-one but an infernal,
rich, plundering old Jew could afford to throw
away good ale! Wot's it all about, Fagin? Damn me,
if my neckerchief ain't lined with beer! What are
you up to? Ill-treating the boys, you covetous,
avaricious, insatiable old fence? I wonder they
don't murder you; I would if I was them. If I'd been
your apprentice I'd have done it long ago, and sold
your body to be stuffed: they'd keep you as a
curiosity of ugliness in a glass bottle – but I
suppose they don't blow bottles big enough for
your nose.

Fagin   Hush, hush, Mister Sikes – don't speak so loud!

Sikes   None of your mistering: you always mean mischief
when you come that. You know my name: out with it!
I shan't disgrace it when the time comes.

Fagin   Well, well, then, Bill Sikes. You seem out of humour,
Bill.

Sikes   So was them wot you just blabbed on, 'cause you
know wot happened to them? They –

Fagin tosses his head towards the Boys.

Fagin   Are you mad?

Sikes shuts up and makes do with miming a hanging.

Sikes	Gimme a glass of liquor. And mind you don't poison it. So what was it all about, Dodger?
Dodger	We've lost a boy to the traps. We'd only had him a day. They grabbed him for stealing an old cove's wipe and hauled him off to the station.
Fagin	And I'm afraid he may say something which will get us into trouble.
Sikes	I should think that's very likely. You're going to be split upon, Fagin!
Fagin	And I'm afraid, you see – I'm afraid that, if the game was up with us, it might be up with a good many more, and that it would come out rather worse for you than it would for me, my dear.
	Sikes spins round furiously: Fagin looks away. Long pause.
Sikes	Somebody must find out wot's been done at that station.
Fagin	Directly.
Sikes	If the boy hasn't peached yet, and is in jail, there's no fear till he comes out again, and then he must be taken care on. You must get hold of him somehow.
Fagin	Very true, very. Someone must go at once.
Dodger	*You* goin', then, Fagin?
Fagin	Why, no, my dear: I'm a little bit too well known, don't you think?
Dodger	Well, oddly enough, I have a violent antipathy to police stations, and I believe Charley here feels the same – don't you, Charley?
Charley	Just a touch.
Dodger	Which don't leave a lot of choice.
Fagin	Nancy, my dear, what do *you* say?
Nancy	That it won't do; so it's no use tryin' it on, Fagin.
Sikes	What do you mean by that?
Nancy	What I say, Bill.

Sikes   Why, you're just the very person for it: nobody around here knows anything about you.

Nancy   And I don't want 'em to, neither. It's rather more no than yes with me, Bill.

Sikes   She'll go, Fagin.

Nancy   No she won't, Fagin.

Sikes   Yes she will, Fagin.

Nancy   Damn your eyes, Bill, I'll not be –

Sikes   Nance. One of us has got to go or none of us is safe. Get her an apron, Charley.

Nancy   Bill –

Sikes   Nance.

Fagin   Here, my dear.

He gives her a little covered basket.

Carry that in one hand. It looks more respectable, my dear.

Sikes   Give her a door-key to carry in her other one, Fagin. It looks real and genuine, like.

Fagin   Yes, yes, my dear, so it does. Very good, very good indeed!

Nancy   Oh my brother! My poor, dear, sweet, innocent little brother! What has become of him? Where have they taken him to? What have they done with my dear little brother – tell me, gentlemen, do!

Nancy exits to thunderous applause.

Fagin   Ah, she's a clever girl, my dears!

Sikes   She's an honour to her sex. Here's her health, and wishing they was all like her!

Music. While Fagin, Sikes and the Boys wait for Nancy to return, the lights dim on them and rise on the other side of the stage.

Scene Thirteen

Lights rise on Brownlow's house, where a Doctor and Mrs Bedwin are leaning over Oliver, sitting in a bath chair.

Oliver   What room is this? Where have I been brought to? This isn't the place I went to sleep in.

Mrs Bedwin   Hush, my dear. You must be very quiet or you'll be ill again; and you've been very bad – as bad as bad could be, pretty nigh.

Doctor   But you're a great deal better now, are you not?

Oliver   Yes, thank you, sir.

Doctor   Yes, I know you are. You're hungry, too, aren't you?

Oliver   No, sir.

Doctor   Ahem. No, I know you're not. He is not hungry, Mrs Bedwin. You feel sleepy, don't you, my dear?

Oliver   No, sir.

Doctor   No, you're not sleepy. Nor thirsty, are you?

Oliver   Yes, sir, rather thirsty.

Doctor   Just as I expected, Mrs Bedwin. It's very natural that he should be thirsty – perfectly natural. You may give him a little tea, ma'am, and some dry toast without any butter. Don't keep him too warm, ma'am; but be careful that you don't let him be too cold. I shall be back tomorrow, ma'am. I shall see myself out. Good day!

Doctor goes.

Oliver   What a beautiful face that lady's is.

Mrs Bedwin   What, my dear?

Oliver   In the picture.

Oliver is gazing at a picture standing on a table nearby.

Mrs Bedwin   Oh. Are you fond of pictures, dear?

Oliver   I don't quite know, ma'am, I have seen so few. Whose likeness is it, ma'am?

Mrs Bedwin	Why really, my dear, I don't know. It's no-one that you or I know, I expect.
Oliver	It is so very pretty.
Mrs Bedwin	Why, sure you're not afraid of it?
Oliver	Oh, no. But the eyes look so sorrowful, and where I sit they seem fixed upon me. It makes my heart beat, as if it was alive, and wanted to speak to me, but couldn't.
Mrs Bedwin	Lord save us! Don't talk like that, child! Let me turn the picture round, and then you won't see it.
Oliver	Oh!

He has seen Mr Brownlow entering, and tries to stand up out of respect: but his legs are too weak and he sinks down.

Brownlow	No, no, no – oh, dear boy, dear boy. You must take care.
Oliver	Yes, sir. Thank you, sir.
Brownlow	How do you feel, my dear?
Oliver	Very happy, sir, and very grateful indeed, sir, for your goodness to me.
Brownlow	Have you given him any nourishment, Bedwin? Eh?
Mrs Bedwin	He has just had a basin of beautiful strong broth, sir.
Brownlow	Ugh! A couple of glasses of port wine would have done him a great deal more good. Wouldn't they, Tom White, eh?
Oliver	My name is Oliver, sir.
Brownlow	Oliver? Oliver what? Oliver White, eh?
Oliver	No, sir, Twist, Oliver Twist.
Brownlow	Queer name! What made you tell the magistrate your name was White?
Oliver	I never told him so, sir.
Brownlow	Oh. Some mistake.
Oliver	I hope you're not angry with me, sir?

Brownlow	No, no. Gracious God, what's this? Bedwin, look, look there!

Brownlow is pointing at the picture of the lady.

The living copy! Look at the boy, Bedwin. The very living copy!

Music. While Mrs Bedwin continues to nurse Oliver, and Fagin and the others continue to wait, the lights rise on a third corner of the stage.

Scene Fourteen

Lights rise on the Police Station: Nancy rushes up to the Officer.

Nancy   Oh, sir, please! You took my poor little brother in this morning. Where is he? Please! I've got to see him!

Officer   *I* haven't got him, dearie.

Nancy   Where is he?

Officer   Why, the gentleman's got him.

Nancy   What gentleman? Oh, gracious heavens! What gentleman?

Officer   The prosecutor. Your brother was taken ill, love; then this bloke comes in and says your brother hadn't done it in the first place; and the gent takes your brother back to his home.

Nancy   Where? Where?

Officer   Somewhere in Pentonville, I heard him say. That's all I can tell you, love.

Nancy   Oh, God!

Officer   Sorry, sweetheart. I'd tell you more if I could.

Nancy rushes out.

Good luck! Hope you find him!

Music. Lights fade on the Officer and brighten on Brownlow's house again.

Scene Fifteen

Lights up on Brownlow's house, where Mrs Bedwin is finishing dressing Oliver in a brand new suit.

Mrs Bedwin Very smart! Mr Brownlow will be proud of you!

Oliver Mrs Bedwin.

Mrs Bedwin Yes, Oliver?

Oliver Where is the picture of the lady?

Mrs Bedwin Ah! It's gone, you see.

Oliver I see it is. Why have they taken it away?

Mrs Bedwin It's been taken away, child, because Mr Brownlow said that as it seemed to worry you perhaps it might prevent your getting well, you know.

Oliver Oh, no, it didn't worry me, ma'am. I liked to see it.

Mr Brownlow and Mr Grimwig enter.

Grimwig Ah! So this is the boy, is it?

Brownlow This is the boy!

Grimwig How are you, boy?

Oliver Much better, thank you, sir.

Brownlow This is an old friend of mine, Oliver – Mr Grimwig. Oliver – go downstairs with Mrs Bedwin and bring up the tea.

Grimwig And muffins.

Brownlow And muffins.

Grimwig Buttered.

Brownlow Buttered.

Oliver Yes, sir.

Oliver and Mrs Bedwin go.

Brownlow He's a nice-looking boy, is he not?

Grimwig I don't know.

Brownlow Don't know?

Grimwig   No. I never see any difference in boys. I only know two sorts of boys: mealy boys and beef-faced boys.

Brownlow And which is Oliver?

Grimwig   Mealy. I know a friend who has a beef-faced boy; a fine boy, they call him; with a round head, and red cheeks, and glaring eyes; a horrid boy; with the voice of a foghorn and the appetite of a wolf. The wretch!

Brownlow Come, these are not the characteristics of Oliver Twist, so he needn't excite your wrath.

Grimwig   No. He may have worse. Where does he come from? Who is he? What is he? He has had a fever. What of that? Fevers are not peculiar to good people, are they? I knew a man who was hung in Jamaica for murdering his master. He had had a fever six times! Have you yet heard a full, true and precise account of the life and adventures of Oliver Twist?

Brownlow I shall hear it tomorrow morning, Grimwig, when he is alone with me.

Grimwig   Hah! I trust your housekeeper counts the plates at night! If she doesn't find a spoon or two missing some sunshiny morning, I shall eat my head, sir, I shall eat my head!

Brownlow I'll answer for that boy's truth with my life!

Grimwig   And I for his falsehood with my head!

Brownlow We shall see!

Grimwig   We shall! Now where are these muffins?

Music. Lights dim on Brownlow and Grimwig and brighten again on Fagin's Den.

Scene Sixteen

Lights rise on Fagin's den. Nancy enters after her visit to the Police Station.

Dodger   She hasn't got him!

Fagin   Nancy! What's happened?

Nancy	The young brat's been ill and the old cove's taken him.
Charley	Why ain't he in the cells?
Nancy	He's been cleared.

Sikes roars and storms out.

Fagin	We must know where he is, my dears; he must be found, or he may lead the law right to us!
Nancy	The old cove lives up Pentonville, they said.
Fagin	Charley, do nothing but skulk about till you bring home news of him! Nancy, my dear, I must have him found. I trust to you, my dear – to you and the Dodger for everything! Stay, stay – there's money, my dears. I shall shut up this shop tonight. You'll know where to find me! Don't stop here a minute. Not an instant, my dears!

Music. Lights fade out on Fagin's den and brighten again on Brownlow's house.

Scene Seventeen

Lights up on Oliver entering with the muffins.

Brownlow	Oh, bother!
Grimwig	What's the matter?
Brownlow	That pile of books. I meant to return them to the book-seller. I particularly wished them returned tonight.
Grimwig	Send Oliver with them. He is sure to deliver them safely.

He smiles ironically.

Oliver	Yes, do let me take them, sir.
Brownlow	But you've only just – You *shall* go, Oliver. There they are. You are to say that you have brought these books back, and that you have come to pay the four pound ten I owe him. This is a five-pound note, so you will have to bring me back ten shillings. Mrs Bedwin will tell you the way.

Oliver	I won't be ten minutes, sir!
	He places the books under his arm, buttons up the bank note in a pocket, bows respectfully and goes.
Brownlow	Let me see; he'll be back in twenty minutes at the longest.
	He takes out his watch and places it on the table.
	It will be dark by that time.
Grimwig	Oh, you really expect him to come back, do you?
Brownlow	Don't you?
Grimwig	No. I do not. The boy has a new suit of clothes on his back, a set of valuable books under his arm and a five-pound note in his pocket. He'll join his old friends the thieves and laugh at you! If ever that boy returns to this house, sir, I'll eat my head!
	Music. While Brownlow and Grimwig wait, the lights dim on them and rise on the other side of the stage.

Scene Eighteen

Lights up on a street. Dodger and Nancy enter and buy baked potatoes from a vendor. Suddenly Oliver enters with the books. He is spotted by Dodger, who points him out to Nancy and then hides.

Nancy	Oh, my dear brother! I've found you!
	She flings herself on Oliver.
Oliver	Don't! Let go of me! Who is it?
Nancy	Oh, my gracious! I've found him! Oh, Oliver!
Oliver	What are you stopping me for?
Nancy	You naughty boy, to make me suffer such distress on your account! Come home, come! Thank heavens, I've found him!
Oliver	Let me go!

Woman	What's the matter, ma'am?
Nancy	It's all right, I'm better now; he ran away, near a month ago, from his parents, who are hard-working and respectable people, and went and joined a set of thieves and nearly broke his mother's heart!
Woman	Young wretch!
Potato-seller	Go home, you little brute!
Oliver	I'm not! I don't know her! I haven't any sister: I'm an orphan; I live at Pentonville!
Woman	Only hear him, how he braves it out!

Oliver kicks out at Nancy and breaks loose.

Nancy	You little villain!

Dodger rushes off to get Sikes. The Potato-seller catches Oliver.

Nancy	Oh, make him come home, there's good people, or he'll kill his father and mother, and break my heart!

Sikes rushes in, followed by Dodger, who hides behind the Potato-seller.

Sikes	What's this? Young Oliver! Come home to your poor mother, you young dog! Come home directly!
Oliver	I don't belong to them! I don't know them! Help! Help!
Sikes	Help? Yes, I'll help you, you young rascal! What books are these? You've been a-stealin' them, have you? Give 'em here!

He grabs them and clouts Oliver on the head with them.

Potato-seller	That's right! Bring him to his senses!
Woman	It'll do him good!
Sikes	He's going to get it! Come on, you young villain!
Oliver	Help me! I don't know them! Help me!

They drag Oliver away. Music. The lights fade, and brighten again on Brownlow and Grimwig.

Scene Nineteen

*Brownlow and Grimwig are still sitting, with the
watch on the table between them. Brownlow looks at
the watch and is perturbed. Grimwig takes a
triumphant bite from a muffin. The lights dim on them,
and as the music ends the lights rise on the other side
of the stage.*

Scene Twenty

*Lights up on Fagin's second den. Fagin and Charley
are waiting. Suddenly Sikes enters, dragging Oliver
by the wrist, followed by Nancy and Dodger.*

Charley   Oh, my wig! my wig! Here he is! Oh, Fagin, look
at him! I can't bear it! Hold me, somebody,
while I laugh it out! Look at his togs, Fagin!
Superfine cloth, and the heavy swell cut! Oh, my
eye! And his books, too! Nothing but a gentleman,
Fagin!

Fagin bows to Oliver while Dodger rifles his pockets.

Fagin   Delighted to see you looking so well, my dear. The
Dodger shall give you another suit, my dear, for
fear you should spoil that Sunday one. Why didn't
you write, my dear, and say you were coming? We'd
have got something warm for supper.

*Charley roars with laughter; Dodger pulls out the five-
pound note.*

Sikes   Hallo. What's that?

Dodger   A fiver.

Fagin grabs the note.

Sikes   That's mine, Fagin.

Fagin   No, no, my dear. Mine, Bill, mine. You shall have the books.

Sikes   If that ain't mine – mine and Nancy's, that is – I'll take the boy back again. Come, hand over, will you?

Fagin   This is hardly fair, Bill – hardly fair, is it, Nancy?

Sikes   Fair or not fair, hand over, I tell you! D'you think Nancy and me has got nothing else to do with our precious time but to go scouting after every young boy as gets grabbed through your bungling? Give it here, you avaricious old skeleton, give it here!

He grabs the note back.

That's for our share of the trouble, and not half enough neither. You can keep the books if you're fond of reading; if you ain't, sell 'em.

Charley   They're very pretty. Beautiful writing, innit, Oliver?

Oliver   They belong to the old gentleman! Please send them back – and the money, too. Keep me here all my life, but please send them back! He'll think I stole them!

Fagin   The boy's right. You're right, Oliver, you're right. He *will* think you've stolen them! Ha! Ha! It couldn't have happened better if we'd chosen our time!

Oliver suddenly bolts for the door. Sikes grabs him and beats him with unnecessary violence.

Nancy   Bill! Leave him be! You'll tear the boy to pieces!

Sikes   Serve him right! Stand off from me or I'll split your skull against the wall!

Nancy   I don't care! I don't care! The boy shan't suffer more, unless you kill me first!

Sikes   Shan't he? I'll soon do that, if you don't keep off.

He flings Nancy to the floor.

The girl's gone mad, I think.

Nancy   No she hasn't; no she hasn't, Fagin, don't think it!

Fagin   Then keep quiet, will you?

Nancy No, I won't do that, neither. What do you think of that?

Fagin So you wanted to get away, did you, Oliver? Eh?

He picks up a club.

Wanted to get assistance; call for the police, eh? We'll cure you of that, my young master!

He raises the club to strike Oliver, but Nancy charges forward and snatches it from him.

Nancy I won't stand by and see it done, Fagin! You've got the boy – what more do you want? Leave him be – leave him be – or I shall put that mark on some of you as will bring me to the gallows before my time.

Fagin Why, Nancy, Nancy, you're more clever than ever tonight. Ha! Ha! My dear, you're acting beautifully!

Nancy Am I? Take care I don't overdo it. You'll be the worse for it, Fagin, if I do. So I tell you in good time to keep clear of me.

Sikes Damn your eyes, Nancy, what do you mean by this? Burn my body! Do you know who you are, and what you are?

Nancy Oh yes, I know all about it!

Sikes Well then keep quiet! Or I'll quiet you for a long time to come.

Nancy laughs hysterically.

You're a nice one to take up the pretty and genteel side! A pretty subject for the child to make a friend of!

Nancy God help me, I am! And I wish I'd been struck dead in the street before I'd lent a hand in bringing him here! He's a thief, a liar, a devil, all that's bad, from this night forth. Isn't that enough for the old wretch, without blows?

Fagin Come, come, Sikes, we must have civil words; civil words, Bill.

Nancy Civil words, you villain? You deserve 'em from me! I thieved for you when I was a child not half as old

as him. And I've been in the same trade and the
same service for twelve years since. Don't you know
it? Speak out! Don't you know it?

Fagin Well, well. And if you have, it's your living.

Nancy Aye, it is! It's my living; and the cold, wet, dirty
streets are my home; and you're the wretch that
drove me to 'em long ago, and that'll keep me there,
day and night, day and night, till I die!

*Nancy rushes at Fagin in fury; Sikes seizes her and
wrestles with her until she faints and collapses.*

Sikes She's all right now.

He lays her down in a corner.

She's uncommon strong in the arms when she's up
in this way.

Fagin It's the worst of having to do with women. But
they're clever, and we can't get on in our line
without 'em. Charley, show Oliver to bed.

Charley I suppose he'd better not wear his best clothes
tomorrow, had he?

Fagin Certainly not, my dear.

Charley Pull off the smart ones, Oliver, and I'll give 'em to
Fagin to take care of. What a lark, eh? Ha! Ha!

Music. Lights fade to black.

Interval

PART TWO

Scene Twenty-One

Music. Lights up on Mrs Mann's parlour at the Junior Workhouse. Mrs Mann is humming contentedly to herself as she carries a tea-tray to her table. She is just about to pour herself a cup when there is a loud knock at the door.

Mrs Mann   Oh, who's that? Some of the old workhouse women dying, I suppose. They always die when I'm about to have tea. Don't stand there letting the draught in! Oh, Mr Bumble!

Bumble   At your service, Mrs Mann.

Mrs Mann   Hard weather, Mr Bumble.

Bumble   Hard indeed, ma'am. We have had to give away five pounds of potatoes and three loaves of bread this very afternoon, and yet them paupers are still not contented.

Mrs Mann   When would they be, Mr Bumble?

Bumble   When indeed! This is the port wine, ma'am, that the board has ordered. I thought you might like a bottle. Real, fresh, genuine port wine, only out of the cask this afternoon, clear as a bell, and no sediment!

Mrs Mann   Oh, thank you indeed, Mr Bumble!

Bumble coughs.

You'll have a very cold walk, Mr Bumble.

Bumble   It blows, ma'am, enough to cut one's ears off.

Mrs Mann   Would you care to take a glass of your port?

Bumble	Oh, well –

He coughs again.

Mrs Mann Sit you down, and take off your coat.

Bumble Indeed, ma'am, thank you, ma'am. You have a cat, ma'am, I believe?

Mrs Mann fetches two glasses from the cupboard.

Mrs Mann And kittens, too, basking in the kitchen by the fire. I am so fond of them, you can't imagine.

Bumble Very nice animals, ma'am, cats. Very domestic.

Mrs Mann pours two glasses of port.

Mrs Mann Oh yes! And they're so fond of their home that it's quite a pleasure, I'm sure.

Bumble Mrs Mann, ma'am, I mean to say this, ma'am; that any cat, or kitten, that could live with you, ma'am, and *not* be fond of its home, must be an ass, ma'am.

Mrs Mann Oh, Mr Bumble!

Bumble It's of no use disguising the facts, ma'am; I would drown it myself, with pleasure.

Mrs Mann Then you're a cruel man, and a very hard-hearted man besides.

Bumble Hard-hearted, ma'am? Hard? Are *you* hard-hearted, Mrs Mann?

Mrs Mann Dear me! What a curious question from a single man! What can you want to know for, Mr Bumble?

Bumble drinks his port, wipes his lips, gets up and embraces her.

Mrs Mann Mr Bumble, Mr Bumble, I shall scream!

Bumble kisses her. She struggles and then yields. Knock at the door. Bumble drops Mrs Mann and she starts dusting things frantically.

Who's there?

An Old Woman enters.

Old Woman If you please, mistress, Old Sally's going fast.

Mrs Mann Well what's that to me? I can't keep her alive, can I?

Old Woman	No, mistress, no-one can. She's past all helping now. But she's troubled in her mind, and she says she's got something to tell you which you must hear. She won't die till you come, mistress.
Mrs Mann	These paupers! They won't even die without annoying their betters.
Bumble	They do it on purpose, ma'am.
Mrs Mann	Mr Bumble, don't go away.

Music. Lights fade.

Scene Twenty-Two

Lights up on a dark, empty room at Fagin's den. Oliver is asleep on the floor, wrapped in an old blanket. Nancy creeps up to him, goes to touch him, but then moves away, gasping for breath. Oliver wakes suddenly.

Oliver	Who's there?
Nancy	Me. Only me.

Oliver lifts up a candle to see her.

Put down the light. It hurts my eyes.

Oliver	Are you ill?
Nancy	God forgive me. I never thought of this.
Oliver	Has something happened? Can I help you? I will if I can.

Nancy rocks and gasps for breath.

Nancy! What is it?

Nancy	I don't know what comes over me sometimes. It's this damp dirty room, I think. Now, Olly dear, are you ready?
Oliver	Ready for what?
Nancy	I've come from Bill. You're to come with me.
Oliver	What for?
Nancy	For no harm.

Oliver I don't believe it.

Nancy Have it your own way. For no good, then.

Oliver All right. I'm ready.

Nancy Look – you can't help yourself. If ever you're to get loose from here, this is not the time. I've saved you from being ill-used once, and I do now, for those who would have fetched you if I had not, would have been far more rough than me. I've promised for your being quiet and silent; if you're not you'll only harm yourself and me, and maybe be my death. Don't let me suffer more. If I could help you I would, but I haven't the power. Hush! Every word from you is a blow for me. Give me your hand! Come on! Your hand!

A short burst of music as they leave the room. Sikes and Fagin appear from the shadows.

Sikes You've got the kid?

Nancy Yes, here he is.

Sikes Did he come quiet?

Nancy Like a lamb.

Sikes Glad to hear it, for the sake of his young carcass.

Fagin He'll be no trouble to you, Bill.

Sikes He'd better not be, or he'll be dead, Fagin – think of that before you send him.

Fagin I've thought it all, Bill – he's the boy for you. It's all arranged about bringing off the swag, is it?

Sikes Never mind the details. Leave the boy with me since you're so set on sending him. See you, Nance.

Nancy looks worried, but realizes she has to go with Fagin, leaving Oliver with Sikes.

Do you know what this is?

He pulls out a pistol. Oliver nods.

Well then, look 'ere. This is powder, that 'ere's a bullet, and this is a little bit of an old 'at for waddin'. Got that?

Oliver   Yes.

Sikes   There. Now it's loaded.

Oliver   Yes, I see it is, sir.

Sikes grabs Oliver's wrist and presses the pistol to his temple.

Sikes   Well, if you speak a word when you're out of doors with me, except when I speak to you, that bullet will be in your head without notice. So if you *do* make up your mind to speak without leave, say your prayers first. Come on, young 'un, and don't lag behind. We've got a long way to cover tonight.

Music. Lights fade.

Scene Twenty-Three

Lights up on the maternity room of the workhouse. In the bed Old Sally is dying. A Young Surgeon is sitting, nonchalantly picking his teeth with a quill. Mrs Mann enters with the Old Woman.

Young Surgeon   Cold night, Mrs Mann.

Mrs Mann   Very cold, very. Now what's this woman got to tell me?

Young Surgeon   Oh, it's all U.P. with her, Mrs Mann.

Mrs Mann   It is, is it?

Young Surgeon   If she lasts ten minutes I shall be surprised. Is she dozing, old lady?

Old Woman nods.

Mrs Mann   Damn me, I thought you said it was urgent! How long have I got to wait?

Old Woman   Not long, mistress. We've none of us long to wait for death. He'll be here soon enough for us all!

Mrs Mann   Hold your tongue, you doting idiot! Can't you wake her?

Old Woman   She'll never wake again but once – and that won't be for long!

Mrs Mann   Long or short, she won't find me here when she does wake. Don't you ever worry me again for nothing! It's no part of my duty to see all the old women in the house die, and I won't, you impudent old harridan! If you make a fool of me again, I'll soon cure you, I warrant you!

She is just about to leave when Old Sally raises herself and stretches out her arms.

Old Sally   Who's that?

Old Woman   Hush! Hush! Lie down! Lie down!

Old Sally   I'll never lie down again alive! I *will* tell her! Come here! Nearer! Let me whisper in your ear.

She grasps Mrs Mann and pulls her down beside her.

Turn them away! Make haste! Make haste!

Mrs Mann waves the Old Woman and the Young Surgeon from the room.

Mrs Mann   Well then? What is it?

Old Sally   Listen. Listen. In this very room – in this very bed – I once nursed a pretty young creature, that was brought into the house with her feet cut and bruised with walking. She gave birth to a boy, and died. Let me think – what was the year again?

Mrs Mann   Never mind the year – what about her?

Old Sally   Ay, what about her? What about – I know! I robbed her, so I did! She wasn't cold, she wasn't cold, I tell you, when I stole it!

Mrs Mann   Stole what, for God's sake?

Old Sally   It! The only thing she had. She wanted clothes to keep her warm, and food to eat; but she had kept it safe. It was gold, I tell you! Rich gold, that might have saved her life!

Mrs Mann	Gold! Go on, go on – what of it? Who was the mother? When was it?
Old Sally	She charged me to keep it safe, but I stole it in my heart when she first showed it to me hanging round her neck; and the child's death, perhaps, is on me besides! They would have treated him better, if they had known it all!
Mrs Mann	Known what? Speak!
Old Sally	The boy grew so like his mother that I could never forget it when I saw his face. Poor girl! Poor girl! Such a gentle lamb!
Mrs Mann	Quick! Quick! Or it may be too late! What was the boy's name?
Old Sally	They called him Oliver. The gold I stole was –
Mrs Mann	Yes, yes; what?

Old Sally rises to a sitting position, her throat rattles, and she falls dead. Mrs Mann gasps with frustration. She prizes Old Sally's hand from her dress and finds that it clasps a locket. She holds it up in astonishment.

Hello. What's this?

Music. Lights fade.

Scene Twenty-Four

Lights up on a garden outside a grand house. Toby Crackit, very dapper, is strolling around in the moonlight filtering through the trees. Suddenly he hears a whispered call:

Sikes	Toby! Toby!
Toby	Bill! Am I glad to see you! Where the Hell have you been? I thought you'd given it up.

Sikes enters, pulling Oliver by the wrist.

Sikes	It's the boy. Been draggin' his heels all the way, damn his eyes!

Toby	Who lumbered you with him?
Sikes	Guess.
Toby	Oh, one of Fagin's, eh?
Sikes	Yeah. I told Fagin I needed a littl'un for the job, and he goes and lands me with Oliver!
Toby	He don't look much like a burglar.
Sikes	You said it! I don't know why, but Fagin was dead set on sending this one.
Toby	Oh, look at him! What an invaluable piece he'll be for the old ladies' pockets in chapel! His mug'll be his fortune to him!
Sikes	That's enough.

A sudden noise from the direction of the house.

	What was that?
Toby	I didn't hear nothing.
Sikes	Right. Have you got the crapes?
Toby	Here you are.

Toby gives Sikes two black neckerchiefs, and Sikes ties one round Oliver's face.

Oliver	What are you doing?
Sikes	What did I tell you? Shut it!
Toby	Right. Who's going first?
Sikes	What's that light on for?
Toby	God knows.
Sikes	We'll have to make a dash across the lawn.
Toby	Right.
Sikes	Go on.
Toby	Right!

Toby scampers across to the house.

	The boy next! Come on, young 'un!
Sikes	Go on.
Oliver	What are you doing?
Sikes	Go on, I say!

Toby   What's the matter with the boy? Don't he know what he's here for? Oh, my life!

Sikes Get over there or I'll strew your brains on the grass.

Oliver Oh, for God's sake let me go! I'll never come near London, never! Have mercy on me, don't make me steal!

Sikes By Christ, I'll –

Sikes cocks his pistol, but Toby rushes across and strikes it from his grasp and claps his hand over Oliver's mouth.

Toby   That's no good, Bill! Listen, young 'un: say another word, and I'll finish you off myself with a crack on the head. That makes no noise, and is just as certain, and more genteel. Come on, Bill. He's game enough now, I reckon.

They all run over to the house.

Sikes Now listen, you young imp. You see that trap-door? I'm putting you through there. You'll find yourself in the cellar of this house. Go softly up the stairs that you'll see straight afore you and round to the street door. Unfasten it, and let us in.

Toby   There's a bolt at the top, you won't be able to reach. Stand on one of the hall chairs. There's three there, Bill, with a jolly blue unicorn and gold lions on 'em –

Sikes Shut it, can't you? The room-door's open, is it?

Toby   Wide. They always leave it open so as the dog can walk in the passage when he's wakeful.

Sikes The dog?!

Toby   Ay! But I enticed him away tonight! Ha! Ha!

Sikes Shut up! Now get to work!

Toby expertly opens the trapdoor with a crowbar.

Toby   It's all yours!

Sikes   Right. Oliver.

Oliver squeezes through the trapdoor.

You see the stairs afore you?

Oliver   Yes.

Sikes   Get to work. Oliver!

Oliver   Yes?

Sikes thrusts his pistol through the trapdoor.

Sikes   You're within shot all the way. Falter once and you're dead. It's done in a minute. Go to it.

A noise from the top of the stairs.

Toby   What was that?

Silence.

Sikes   Nothing. Now, Oliver.

Oliver hesitates, then goes. Suddenly a loud noise and light from the top of the stairs.

Sikes   Come back! Back! Back!

Oliver freezes in panic, then tries to get back through the trapdoor. Shouts. Gunshots. Oliver is hit.

Oliver   AAAHHH!

Music. Sikes grabs him and pulls him back through the trapdoor.

Sikes   Clasp your arm tighter! Give me a shawl here! They've hit him! Quick! Damnation, how the boy bleeds!

A bell rings. Shouting. Toby and Sikes flee, Sikes dragging Oliver.

Sikes   Stop, you white-livered hound! Stop! Give me a hand with the boy! Toby!

Toby   It's all up, Bill! Drop the kid and show 'em your heels!

Sikes   Shaa!

*He drops Oliver and runs. The music stops. A Servant
rushes on with a gun.*

Servant They've run! They've legged it across the field!

Grimwig runs on, followed by his daughter, Rose.

Grimwig Keep your head down! They may take a parting shot!
Ah! Giles! Look here!

Servant What's that? Oh, here he is! Here's one of the
thieves, miss! Wounded, miss! I shot him, miss! Don't
be frightened, I'm all right: he didn't make a very
desperate resistance, miss!

Rose It's a boy!

Grimwig Well I'll be –

Rose What is it, father?

Grimwig If it isn't little Oliver I'll eat my head!

Rose You know him, father?

Grimwig Twist. Oliver Twist. I told him! I told old Brownlow
all along! The boy's a villain and a thief. I should
have had a wager on it!

Rose He's bleeding terribly, poor child.

Grimwig Poor child? Ha! Haul him into the house, Giles. I'm
going to fetch Brownlow before I call for the police.
His face will be a picture! 'Pon my soul! His innocent
little angel! Just a common little thief!

Music. Lights fade.

Scene Twenty-Five

*Lights up on Fagin's second den. Fagin is pacing,
reading a newspaper. Dodger and Charley are playing
cards. Suddenly Charley throws down his cards in
disgust.*

Charley That's two doubles and the rub! I never see such a
feller as you, Dodger. You win everything. Even when
I get good cards I can't make nothing of 'em. Shaa!

Fagin	What's the matter, Charley?
Charley	Matter, Fagin? I wish you'd watched the play. I ain't won a blessed point.
Fagin	Ay, ay! Well, try 'em again, Charley, try 'em again!
Charley	No more of it for me, thank you, Fagin. I've had enough. That 'ere Dodger has had such a run of luck that there's no chance against him.

Dodger is producing cards from his sleeves behind Charley's back.

Fagin	Ha, ha, my dear! You must get up very early in the morning to win against the Artful!
Charley	Morning! You must keep your boots on overnight if you want to come over him. What're you laughin' at, Fagin?
Dodger	How precious dull you are, Charley!
Charley	What?
Dodger	Hark! I heard the tinkler.
Fagin	See if it's them. Quick!
Dodger	It's Toby.
Fagin	What! Alone?

Toby enters.

Toby	How are you, Faguey?
Fagin	Toby –
Toby	See there, Faguey –

He points to his boots.

Not a drop of Day and Martin since you know when; not a bubble of blackin', by Jove! Don't look at me in that way, man. All in good time. I can't talk about business till I've eat and drank; so produce the sustainance, and let's have a quiet fill-out for the first time in three days!

Fagin gestures to Dodger and Charley to bring food and drink. Toby complacently starts his meal.

Fagin	Speak out, Toby! You're settled now!
Toby	There's time enough.

Fagin No be God there ain't! Speak out!
Toby cockily dabs his lips.
Toby First and foremost, Faguey –
Fagin Yes, yes.
Toby takes a swig of drink.
Toby This gin is excellent. First and foremost, Faguey, how's Bill?
Fagin What!
Toby Why, you don't mean to say –
Fagin Mean? Where are they? Sikes and the boy! Where are they? Where have they been? Why have they not been here?
Toby The crack failed.
Fagin I knew it!
He tears out a newspaper and points to it.
What more?
Toby They fired and hit the boy. We cut over the fields at the back, with him between us – straight as the crow flies – through hedge and ditch. They gave chase. Damn me! The whole country was awake, and the dogs upon us!
Fagin The boy!
Toby Bill had him on his back and scuddled like the wind. We stopped to take him between us; his head hung down, and he was cold. They were hard on our heels. Every man for himself, and each from the gallows! We split up, and left the youngster lying in a ditch. Alive or dead, that's all I know about him.
Fagin screams.
Charley Lumme.
Toby Why's the boy so important?
Fagin I've got to have him back!
Toby He's probably dead in a ditch!
Fagin I've got to have him back! Dodger, go and find him.
Dodger Who? Oliver?
Fagin No, you know who.
Dodger Here, you don't mean –

Fagin	Monks.
Dodger	Monks! I ain't goin' near him!
Fagin	He's got to know! Tell him to come here tomorrow night without fail. Tell him it's about the boy. You're going, Dodger!
Dodger	Am I ever!

Fagin takes him in a terrible grip.

Fagin	You're going, Dodger!
Dodger	All right! All right! I'll go!
Fagin	Make haste.
Dodger	Where are *you* going?
Fagin	To Bill's house. He's got to be back! He's got to be!

Fagin rushes out.

Charley	Lumme.
Toby	What's so important about the blessed boy?

Music. Lights fade.

Scene Twenty-Six

Lights up on Sikes's house. Nancy is slumped over the table with an empty gin bottle in front of her. Fagin enters.

Fagin Nancy. Nancy! It's Fagin.

No reply. He picks up the empty bottle.

She's been drinking.

To himself.

Now if there's any deep play here, my girl, I shall have it out of you, cunning as you are.

He bangs the bottle on the table.

Nancy!

She comes to with a start and looks up, but then lets her head sink again.

Where should you think Bill was now, my dear?

Nancy How can I tell?

Fagin And the boy, too. Poor little child! Left in a ditch, Nancy! Only think!

Nancy The child is better where he is than among us. I hope that he lies dead in the ditch, and that his young bones may rot there.

Fagin What!

Nancy Ay, I do! I shall be glad to have him away from my eyes, and to know that the worst is over. I can't bear to have him about me. The sight of him turns me against myself and all of you.

Fagin Pooh! You're drunk!

Nancy Am I? It'd be no fault of yours if I wasn't! You'd never have me anything else if you had your way, except now; the humour doesn't suit you, does it?

Fagin No! It doesn't!

Nancy Change it, then!

Fagin Change it! I *will* change it! Listen to me, you drab. Listen to me, who with six words can strangle Sikes as surely as if I had his bull's throat between my fingers now. If he comes back and leaves the boy behind him, if he gets off free and fails to restore the boy to me, you'd better murder him yourself if you want him to escape the hangman!

Nancy What is all this?

Fagin What is it? When the boy's worth hundreds of pounds to me, am I to lose him through the bungling of a drunken gang?

Nancy Oliver? Worth hundreds of pounds? What do you mean?

Fagin Nothing, Nancy. Nothing at all. I was –

A noise on the stairs.

Bill!

Nancy Bill!

They both go towards the door. Monks enters.

Fagin Monks!

Monks I've been looking for you all night. What are you doing here?

Fagin Business, my dear. *Your* business, *your* business.

Monks It's not *her* business. Get her out of here.

Nancy sits on the bed defiantly.

Fagin Nancy. Nancy, this isn't the time –

Nancy goes.

Monks Shut the door. You've seen the paper?

Fagin The crack failed.

Monks But the boy – was it Oliver?

Fagin Monks –

Monks Did you send Oliver? Did you?

Fagin I did, my dear.

Monks And left him there! You left him there!

Fagin Not me! Sikes! And flash Toby Crackit!

Monks Why send him on a job like that?

Fagin We'll get him back, my dear.

Monks Why could you not keep him here among the rest, and make a sneaking, snivelling pickpocket of him?

Fagin Only hear him!

Monks Haven't you done it with other boys scores of times? If you'd had patience for a month or two couldn't you have got him convicted and sent safely out of the kingdom; perhaps for life?

Fagin It was not easy to train him to the business. He was not like other boys in the same circumstances.

Monks Curse him, no! Or he would have been a thief long ago.

Fagin I had no hold upon him to make him worse: his hand was not in. I had nothing to frighten him with, which we must always have in the beginning or we labour in vain. What could I do? Just send him out with

the Dodger and Charley? Look what happened when
we did that! Disaster! Arrested in ten minutes!

Monks I'll not quarrel with that. If it had never happened I
might never have clapped eyes upon him and
realized it was him I was looking for. And you showed
some talent in getting him back.

Fagin Quite so, my dear! Now, you want Oliver made a thief.
If he is alive, I can make him one from this time; and if
– if – it's not likely, mind – but if the worst comes to
the worst, and he is dead –

Monks It's no fault of mine if he is! Mind that, Fagin! I had no
hand in it. Anything but his death, I told you from the
first. I won't shed blood; it's always found out, and
haunts a man besides. If they shot him dead, I was
not the cause, do you hear me?

*Nancy dashes in behind them and hides behind the
bed.*

Fire this infernal den! What was that?

Fagin What! Where?

Monks Yonder! I saw the shadow of a woman pass across the
doorway like a breath!

They rush up to the staircase.

Fagin Nancy! Nancy!

Silence.

She's not there. It's your fancy. She's gone out for
more gin.

Monks I'll swear I saw it. It was bending forward when I saw
it first; and when I spoke it darted away.

Fagin There's no-one in the house besides ourselves. It's
past one o'clock. What's the next move, Monks?

Monks You do all in your power to find the boy, be he dead
or alive. And I have some evidence to destroy.

Fagin Evidence, my dear?

Monks   You handle your business, I'll handle mine. Be about it.

Fagin   As you say, my dear, as you say. Good night.

Monks   I hardly think so.

Monks leaves. After a moment Fagin follows. Music. Nancy emerges from her hiding-place and snatches up the newspaper left behind by Monks. The lights fade on Nancy reading urgently.

Scene Twenty-Seven*

As the music ends, lights rise on a room in Grimwig's house. Brownlow hurries in.

Brownlow   Bring the boy into the back room! There are two constables coming up the drive! We must sort this out before we see the police!

Grimwig and Rose hurry in with Oliver.

Now, Oliver, you say they forced you to it?

Oliver   Yes, sir, upon my word. Mr Sikes dragged me here in the dead of night, and I didn't know what it was for until they – they drew out their masks and pistols, sir. Then they pushed me through the – through the –

Brownlow   The trap-door.

Oliver   Yes. And I remember nothing more. And now I – please, I –

Grimwig   He's a fine actor!

Brownlow   You don't believe his tale?

Grimwig   Ha! He span us a handsome yarn before! You'll not be fooled again?

Ring of the doorbell.

---

*If following the doubling scheme given in the cast list, so that **Grimwig** and **Monks** are played by the same actor, see p. 90 for alternative Scene 27.

Rose	They're here!
Brownlow	I *will* be fooled again! If it means the boy can be safe and well I *will* be fooled again! If the police arrest him he'll be dead in a week. Rose, let the constables in. Give them your report about the burglary, but say nothing about the boy.
Grimwig	Brownlow!
Brownlow	He's ill, man! And I believe him – twice, yes, I believe him! I'm taking Oliver home to Pentonville. And you'll have to eat your head!

Music. Lights fade.

Scene Twenty-Eight

Lights up on a public house. Mr Bumble is sitting with a newspaper and a pot of ale. Monks enters as the music ends, sees him, and joins him at his table.

Monks	Mr Bumble. You are the beadle here, are you not?
Bumble	I am, sir. Parochial beadle.
Monks	And have been these fifteen years.
Bumble	Sixteen, sir. Sixteen this very week! Oh, you must be –
Monks	You don't know my name. I would recommend you not to ask for it.
Bumble	I meant no harm, young man.
Monks	And have done none. You have the same eye to your own interest that you always had, I doubt not?

Bumble looks astonished.

Don't scruple to answer freely, man. I know you pretty well, you see.

Bumble	I am not averse to earning an honest penny when I can.
Monks	Now listen to me. I came down to this village today, to find you out; and by one of those chances

that the devil throws in the way of his friends sometimes, I walk into the very room you're sitting in while you are uppermost in my mind. Be quick in answering what I ask you, for I want to reach the place I am to sleep in before the cursed black night comes on. Do you understand me?

Bumble   I hear you, but to say I understood you, you know, would be rather stretching the point at present.

Monks   I shall be plain enough. I want some information from you. I don't ask you to give it for nothing, slight as it is. Put up that, to begin with.

He pushes two sovereigns towards Bumble.

Carry your memory back – let me see – twelve years last winter.

Bumble   It's a long time. Very good. I've done it.

Monks   The scene, the workhouse.

Bumble   Good!

Monks   And the time, night.

Bumble   Yes.

Monks   And the place, the crazy hole in which miserable women gave birth to whining children for the parish to rear, and hide their own shame, God rot 'em, in the grave!

Bumble   The maternity room, I suppose?

Monks   Yes. A boy was born there.

Bumble   Many boys!

Monks   Curse 'em! I speak of one; a meek-looking, pale-faced hound, who was apprenticed down here to a coffin-maker – I wish he had made *his* coffin and screwed his body in it – and who afterwards ran away to London.

Bumble   Why, you mean Oliver! Young Twist! I remember him, of course! There wasn't an obstinater young rascal –

Monks   It's not of him I want to hear. It's of a woman – the hag that nursed his mother. Where is she?

Bumble   Where is she? It would be hard to tell. There won't be a workhouse there, whichever place she's gone to!

Monks   What do you mean?

Bumble   That she died last winter.

Long pause.

Monks   Well. No matter, then, no matter.

Bumble   There was a woman, though. … No, no.

Monks   What?

Bumble   Well, there was a woman who was closeted with the old hag shortly before she died, and she had something to tell her with her last words. Something terrible important, so it seemed.

Monks   How can I find her?

Bumble   Only through me.

Monks   When?

Bumble   Tomorrow.

Monks   At nine in the evening, at nine in the evening, bring her to me there. I needn't tell you to be secret.

He hands Bumble a scrap of paper and starts to go at once.

Bumble   Er –

He goes and touches Monks on the arm.

Monks   What do you want?

Bumble   Only to ask a question. What name am I to ask for?

Monks   Monks! We have separate ways. Don't follow me. Now go!

Music. Lights fade.

Scene Twenty-Nine

Lights up on a derelict house by the Thames. Sounds of rain and rumbling water. Mrs Mann enters with a lantern.

Mrs Mann   This can't possibly be the place! Bumble, let me see the paper. Where are you, Bumble?

Bumble	Here, my sweet. Could have sworn I put it in me waistcoat pocket.
Mrs Mann	God in Heaven, you haven't lost it? The man's an imbecile.
Bumble	No, no, my pigeon. Here it is.
Mrs Mann	Gracious God, it *is* the place. He must be a respectable sort.

Monks suddenly emerges from the dark.

Monks	Is this the woman?

Bumble leaps out of his skin.

Bumble	Oh, my God! Ah – yes – this is she.

Crash of thunder.

Monks	Hear it! Hear it! Rolling and crashing on as if it echoed through Hell. Fire the sound! I hate it! These fits come over me now and then, and thunder sometimes brings them on. Don't mind me now; it's all over for this once. Now, the sooner we come to our business the better for all. The woman knows what it is, does she?
Mrs Mann	Yes.
Monks	He is right in saying that you were with this hag the night she died; and that she told you something –
Mrs Mann	About the mother of Oliver Twist. Yes.
Monks	The first question is, of what nature was her communication?
Mrs Mann	That's the second question. The first is, what may the communication be worth?
Monks	How the devil do I know, without knowing of what kind it is?
Mrs Mann	You had better bid.
Monks	Is it about something that was taken from her – something that she wore?
Mrs Mann	Give me five and twenty pounds in gold and I'll tell you all I know.
Monks	Five and twenty pounds!
Mrs Mann	It's not a large sum.

Monks   For a paltry secret that may be nothing when it's told!

Mrs Mann   You can easily take it away again if it is. I am but a woman, alone here and unprotected.

Bumble   I am here, my dear.

Mrs Mann   You are a fool. Hold your tongue.

Monks   Here.

He lays out twenty-five sovereigns.

Gather them up. And when this cursed peal of thunder, which I can feel coming up, is gone, let's hear your story.

Loud crash of thunder. Monks again clutches himself to suppress a fit.

Mrs Mann   When this woman, that we called Old Sally, died, she and I were alone.

Monks   There was no-one else by? No-one who could hear, and possibly understand?

Mrs Mann   Not a soul. We were alone. I stood alone beside her body when death came over it.

Monks   Good. Go on.

Mrs Mann   She spoke of a young creature who had brought a child into the world some years before; not merely in the same room, but in the same bed in which she then lay dying.

Monks   Ay? Blood, how things come about!

Mrs Mann   The child was the one you named to him last night – Oliver Twist; the mother Old Sally had robbed.

Monks   In life?

Mrs Mann   In death. She stole from the corpse what the dead mother had begged her to keep for Oliver's sake.

Monks   Did she sell it? Did she sell it?

Mrs Mann   As she told me that she had stolen it, she fell back and died.

Monks   Without saying more? It's a lie! I'll not be played with! She said more! I'll tear the life out of you both, but I'll know what it was!

Mrs Mann   She didn't utter another word. But she

clutched my gown violently with one hand, which was partly closed; and when I saw that she was dead and removed the hand by force, I found it clasped a locket.

Monks   Where is it now? Where is it?

Mrs Mann   There.

She throws down a little pouch. Monks pounces on it. There is a locket inside.

It has the word Agnes engraved on the inside.

Monks chuckles.

Listen, young man: I don't know anything about all this, beyond what I can guess at, and I don't want to know, for it's safer not to. But just tell me this: is that all you expected to get from me?

Monks   It is. Come here.

Mrs Mann   Why is the locket so important?

Monks   Never you mind! Come here!

Mr Bumble and Mrs Mann move up onto a platform.

Don't move another step forward, or your life is not worth a bulrush.

A burst of music. He throws open a large trapdoor at Bumble's feet. Bumble leaps back. There is a loud roar of water from beneath.

Look down. If you flung a man's body down there, where would it be tomorrow morning?

Bumble   Twelve miles down the river, and cut to pieces besides.

Another burst of music. Monks drops the pouch with the locket down the trap, then slams it shut.

Monks   There. We have nothing more to say, and may break up our pleasant party.

Bumble	By all means.
Monks	You'll keep a quiet tongue in your head, will you? I'm not afraid of the woman here.
Bumble	You may depend on me, Mr Monks.
Monks	You may as well teach yourself to drop that name, do you mind?
Bumble	Certainly.
Monks	And if we meet again anywhere, there's no call for us to know each other – you understand?
Bumble	Quite, quite.
Monks	I'm glad to hear it, for your sake. Now get away from here as fast as you can.

Music. Lights fade.

Scene Thirty

Lights up on Sikes's house. Sikes is ill in bed, sweating and feverish. Nancy is giving him a dose of laudanum. She mops his brow, then checks that he is falling asleep and goes to put on her shawl. Fagin and Dodger enter.

Fagin	Bill, my dear, how are you?

Sikes wakes suddenly.

Sikes	Fagin! Where the devil have you been? What do you mean by leaving a man in this state for three weeks and more, you false-hearted vagabond?
Fagin	Only hear him, Dodger! And us come to bring him all these beautiful things!
Dodger	A rabbit pie, Bill, the very bones will melt in your mouth! Piece of Double Gloster, and the richest sort you ever lushed!
Sikes	Hold your din. What have you got to say for yourself, you withered old fence, eh? Where the Hell

have you been?

Fagin   We've had to move, Bill, with the boy being caught. Heaven knows what he might have told the law.

Sikes   Listen, Fagin. I caught the ague in your service, splashing about in the fields after that burglary, and it nearly cost me my neck, and you leave me here to starve and dwindle for three weeks. If it hadn't been for Nance I might have died.

Nancy   He says true enough there, God knows. Now leave him be.

Dodger   Don't he want a piece of pie?

Nancy   I've just given him laudanum – he'll be out cold in a moment. Leave him be.

Nancy waits for them to go, but they stay put. Sikes is drifting into sleep. Nancy picks up her shawl and hat.

Fagin   Where are you going, my dear?

Nancy   Out for a breath of air.

Fagin   But you're looking after Bill.

Nancy   *You're* here now, and can make up for the three weeks. He'll be no trouble to you – look, he's gone already.

Fagin   Very well, my dear. Very well. When will you be back?

Nancy   You won't have to suffer long – don't vex yourself.

She goes.

Fagin   It's not like Nancy to slip off like that. Where can she be going?

Dodger   Beats me.

Music. While Dodger and Fagin sit with the sleeping Sikes, the lights dim on them and rise on the other side of the stage.

Scene Thirty-One

The front door of a hotel. Nancy, after a furtive approach to make sure she has not been followed, comes up to the Doorman.

Doorman Now, young woman, what do you want here?

Nancy A lady who is stopping at this here hotel.

Doorman A lady? What lady?

Nancy Her name is Rose.

Doorman Oh, yeah? What name am I to say?

Nancy It's no use saying any – she don't know me.

Doorman What's your business?

Nancy Never mind that. I must see the lady.

Doorman Hey! None of this! Take yourself off.

Nancy You'll have to carry me out! And I can make that a job that two of you won't like to do! Please, just take a message – say it's about Oliver Twist and she'll come. For God Almighty's sake take my message!

Doorman Here, keep your voice down! This ain't Whitechapel, you know. This is a respectable neighbour'ood. I'll get her. She'll see you out here – you ain't comin' in like that. Don't budge.

He goes and returns in a moment with Rose.

This is the woman, ma'am.

Nancy It's a hard matter getting to see you, lady. But you'll be glad I stayed.

Rose It's about Oliver.

Nancy Yes, lady.

Rose Go on.

Nancy It must be in private.

Rose (*to Doorman*) Would you?

Doorman Are you sure, ma'am? Very well.

He goes.

Rose What is it?

Nancy I am about to put my life, and the lives of others, in your hands. I'm the girl that dragged little Oliver back to old Fagin's, the Jew's, on the night he left the house in Pentonville with the books.

Rose You!

Nancy I, lady! I'm the infamous creature you'll have heard of, that lives among the thieves. But I've stolen away from those who would surely murder me if they knew I'd been here, to tell you what I've overheard. Do you know a man named Monks?

Rose No.

Nancy Well he knows you, and he knows that you're here, for it was by hearing him tell of this hotel that I found you out.

Rose Monks? I never heard the name.

Nancy Then he goes by more than one name, as I've long suspected. Some time ago, and soon after Oliver was forced to take part in burgling your father's house, I overheard a conversation between Monks and Fagin in the dark. I found out that Monks had struck a bargain with Fagin, that if Fagin could get Oliver back he would get a big reward; and he was to have an even bigger one for making Oliver a thief, which this Monks wanted for some purpose of his own.

Rose For what purpose?

Nancy I never found out. Monks caught sight of my shadow on the wall as I listened, so I heard no more. But I saw Monks again last night.

Rose And what happened then?

Nancy I'll tell you, lady. Last night he and Fagin met again. They didn't know it, but I was listening at the door. The first words I heard Monks say were these:

Music. In a corner of the stage in a pool of strange light, Monks meets Fagin.

Monks I dropped the locket down the trap. So the only proof of Oliver's identity lies at the bottom of the river, and the old hag that received it from his mother is rotting in her coffin!

Nancy They laughed, and talked of his success in doing

this; and Monks, talking on about Oliver and getting very wild, said:

Monks I've got the young devil's money safely now: now it all comes to me! But I'd rather have got it by making him a thief! What a game it would have been to have dragged him through every jail in the town, and then had him hanged for some capital offence!

Rose What is all this?

Nancy The truth, lady. Then he said:

Monks If I could take Oliver's life without bringing my own neck in danger, I would. But as I can't I'll be there to meet him at every turn in his life. In short, Fagin, you never laid such snares as I'll contrive for my young brother Oliver!

Music stops and Monks and Fagin disappear.

Rose His brother!

Nancy Those were his words. I must get back now, quickly, or they'll suspect me.

Rose Go back? To men you paint in such terrible colours?

Nancy I must, because – how can I tell such things to an innocent lady like you? – because among the men I've told you of, there is one – the most desperate of them all – that I can't leave, no, not even to be saved from the life I'm leading now. I couldn't be his death!

Rose Why should you be?

Nancy If I told others what I've told you, and led to their being taken, he'd be sure to hang. He is the boldest, and has been so cruel!

Rose Then why stay with him? It's madness!

Nancy I don't know what it is – but it's the same with hundreds of others as wretched as me. Whether it's God's wrath for the wrong I've done I don't know, but I'm drawn back to Bill whatever he makes me suffer.

And I think I would be, even if I knew I was to die by his hand.

Rose   But you can't go now: how will your telling me all this help Oliver, if it's not followed up and pursued?

Pause.

Nancy   I'll meet you again – there isn't time now – and you must bring the gentleman who rescued Oliver the first time. On Sunday night, from eleven until the clock strikes twelve, I'll walk on London Bridge if I'm alive.

Rose   Stay – take some money from me at least.

Nancy   Not a penny.

Rose   Please let me help you!

Nancy   You would help me best, lady, if you took my life at once; for I feel more grief to think of what I am tonight than I ever did before, and it would be something not to die in the Hell in which I've lived. God bless you, lady, and send as much happiness on your head as I've brought shame on mine! London Bridge – Sunday night – between eleven and twelve!

Nancy hurries away. Music. The lights fade on Rose and brighten again on Sikes's house.

Scene Thirty-Two

Sikes's house. Sikes is sitting up in bed. Nancy is pacing nervously.

Fagin   You seem on edge, Nancy, my dear.

Nancy   Do I? What time is it?

Fagin feels in his pocket. No watch. Dodger whisks it from his own pocket.

Dodger   Just a little practice! Soon be eleven.

Sikes   Dark and heavy it is, too. A good night for business, this.

Fagin	You'll soon be back at it, Bill, my dear. You're getting righter by the day.
Dodger	Then you can make up for the lost time.
	Nancy is putting on her shawl and bonnet.
Sikes	Hello! Nance! Where's the girl going to this time of night?
Nancy	Not far.
Sikes	What answer's that? Where are you going?
Nancy	I say not far.
Sikes	And I say where? Do you hear me?
Nancy	I don't know where!
Sikes	Then I do. Nowhere. Sit down.
Nancy	I'm not well. I told you that before. I want a breath of air.
Sikes	Stick your head out of the winder.
Nancy	There's not enough there. I want it in the street.
Sikes	Then you won't have it.
	He pulls off her shawl and bonnet.
	There! Now sit down. Nice and quiet.
Nancy	Bill!
Sikes	You heard!
	She does as he says. Music. Lights dim on Sikes's house and rise on the other side of the stage where Brownlow and Rose appear on the bridge. They wait.
Brownlow	Not a soul. Between eleven and twelve, she said? I hope she's not long. It's a filthy night.
	They wait. Music. Lights shift back to Sikes's house. Sikes has gone to sleep. Nancy is looking anxious. Fagin whispers to her.
Fagin	Nancy, my dear, Bill's asleep. Why don't you slip out for a while if you want your breath of air?

Nancy	What if he wakes?
Fagin	I'll talk him round. Go on, my dear, don't worry yourself.
Nancy	Thanks, Fagin. You're a pal.
	She grabs her shawl and slips out.
Fagin	Now, Dodger! Follow her! Watch her every step!
	Dodger dashes out. Music. Lights shift back to the bridge.
Brownlow	Five to midnight. She isn't going to come. We may as well go.
Rose	Just five minutes more! She'll come if she can, I know she will.
Brownlow	I'm chilled to the marrow. Come.
Rose	Please wait!
Brownlow	It's hopeless, Rose. Come. Come.
	They start to go. Suddenly Nancy enters.
Nancy	Lady!
Rose	She's here!
Nancy	Is this the gentleman?
Brownlow	You've come. We were giving up hope. Quickly. What have you to tell us?
Nancy	God help me.
Brownlow	What is it?
Nancy	I don't know why it is, but I have such a fear and dread upon me tonight that I can hardly stand.
Brownlow	A fear of what?
Nancy	I wish I knew. Horrible thoughts of death, and shrouds with blood upon them, have been on me all day.
	Dodger creeps up to within earshot.
	I was reading a book tonight, and the same things came into the print.
Brownlow	Imagination.

Nancy	No imagination. I'll swear I saw 'coffin' written on every page in large black letters – aye, and a coffin was carried close past me in the street just now.
Brownlow	There's nothing unusual in that. They have passed me often.
Nancy	Real ones. This was not.
Rose	What was that?

She moves towards Dodger's hiding-place.

Nancy	We can't talk here. Come away – down these steps! Come on!

They go. Dodger watches, then slips off after them. Music. Lights shift back to Sikes's house. Sikes stirs in his bed. Dodger and Fagin suddenly burst in.

Fagin	Bill! Bill! Bill!
Sikes	What's up? What are you looking at me like that for?

Fagin is quivering, speechless.

Damn me! He's gone mad!

Fagin	Oh, Bill, Bill, I've got that to tell you as will make you worse than me!
Sikes	Aye? Well tell away, and look sharp.
Fagin	Bill! Nancy, Bill, Nancy!
Sikes	Speak, will you! Open your mouth and say what you've got to say!
Fagin	Suppose the Dodger, Bill, suppose the Artful was to peach – to split on us all – to steal out at nights to find those most bent against us and peach to them. Do you hear me? Suppose he did all this, what then?
Sikes	I'd grind his skull under the iron heel of my boot into as many grains as there are hairs on his head. I'd smash his head as if a loaded waggon had gone over it.
Fagin	What if *I* did it! Or Charley, or even flash Toby Crackit!
Sikes	I don't care who, I'd serve 'em the same!

Fagin Dodger, Dodger, poor lad, he's tired, tired with watching for *her* so long – watching for *her*, Bill.

Sikes What d'yer mean?

Fagin Tell me it again, Dodger – again, just for Bill to hear.

Dodger Fagin, no –

Fagin Tell him, Dodger, tell him about Nancy.

He seizes Sikes by the wrist.

You followed her?

Dodger Yes.

Fagin To London Bridge?

Dodger Yes.

Fagin Where she met two people?

Dodger So she did.

Fagin A gentleman and a lady, who asked her to tell of all her pals, and Monks first, which she did, and to describe him, which she did, and tell what public house we meet in, which she did, and where it could best be watched from, which she did, and what time the people went there, which she did. She did all this. She told it all, every word, of her own free will – did she not?

Dodger She did! She did!

Sikes Hell's fire! Let me go!

Fagin Bill! Bill!

Sikes Let me go! Don't speak to me! It's not safe! Let me go, I say!

Fagin Bill! You won't be – you won't be too violent, Bill? Not too violent for safety. Be crafty, Bill, be crafty!

Sikes Get out of here! Both of you! Get out!

Fagin and Dodger go. Nancy is outside the door, and meets them on their way out.

Nancy Are you going? Goodnight. Till tomorrow.

Long pause. Nancy enters the room.

Oh, Bill, you're up. I thought you'd be asleep. I've been walking for an age, ain't I?

He takes off her bonnet.

Oh, thank you, kind sir!

He takes off her shawl.

The sun's nearly up. I'll draw the curtain.

Sikes   Let it be. There's light enough for what I've got to do.

Nancy   Bill. Why do you look at me like that?

Sikes looks at her, then grasps her by the head and throat and places his hand upon her mouth.

Bill! Bill! I – I won't scream or cry – not once – speak to me! Tell me what I've done!

Sikes   You know, you she-devil! You were watched tonight; every word you said was heard!

Nancy   Then spare my life, for God's sake, as I've spared yours tonight! Bill, Bill, stop before you spill my blood! I've been true to you, upon my guilty soul I have! Bill! The lady and gent I saw tonight offered me an escape – a home abroad! Let's both go and leave this dreadful place and lead better lives away from here! It's never too late, Bill! Bill! No!

Music. Sikes strangles Nancy, forcing her to the ground in a heap. He crawls aside, gasping for air. Suddenly Nancy starts to rise up, staring at Sikes.

Nancy   God have mercy on me!

Sikes screams in horror, smothers her face with her shawl, and snatches up a cudgel. Music and blackout as he brings it down towards her head.

Scene Thirty-Three

*Lights up on Fagin's first den. Dodger is there alone,
agitated, racing through a newspaper. Charley bursts
in.*

Charley   Dodger! Dodger, they've got Fagin! The police have
got Fagin!

Dodger   I know it!

Charley   What are we going to do?

Dodger   It's all acause of Sikes. We warned him not to!

Charley   *He* split on Fagin?

Dodger   *He* killed Nancy! They found her body and raised the
hue and cry. The whole town went barmy and went
hunting in a pack.

Charley   Sikes killed Nancy? What for?

Dodger   She split on the lot of us.

Charley   Oh God! Where is he now?

Dodger   How should I know? They're looking for him
everywhere. A hundred pound reward. They ain't
found him but they've found Fagin! God in Heaven!
What a smash!

Charley   I saw them take Fagin. You should have heard the
people scream at him! The officers fought like devils
to hold 'em back or they'd have torn him to pieces.
They were all jumping up, one behind the other, and
snarling with their teeth and going at him. I can see
him now – the blood on his hair and beard, and the
women swearing they'd tear his heart out!

Dodger   God help us!

Knocking at the door.

What's that? You wasn't followed here, was you?
Charley!

Charley   No! No!

Dodger   Well who is it, then?

Charley   How should I know?

Knocking again.

Dodger   Here – it couldn't be –

Charley   Who?

Dodger   Sikes!

Charley   God Almighty. What are we going to do?

Dodger   We'll have to let him in.

Charley   No chance.

Dodger   Go on. It'll be the worse for us if we don't. Charley, go on.

Charley goes and opens up. Dodger picks up a knife from the stove and hides it inside his coat. Sikes comes in. Silence.

Sikes   Tonight's paper says that Fagin's been took. Is it true, or a lie?

Dodger   True.

Silence.

Sikes   Damn you all! Have you nothing to say to me?

Silence.

The body – the body – is it buried? It's got to be! What do they leave such ugly things above ground for? I can see her eyes. Still staring at me. There! There! As fresh as blood!

Charley starts to move.

Where are you going?

Charley   Let me go into the next room.

Sikes   Charley, don't you – don't you know me?

Charley   Don't come near me! You monster! Dodger – Dodger – I'm not afraid of him – if they come here after him I'll give him up – I will! I tell you that straight! He can kill me for it if he likes, but if I'm here I'll give him up! I'd give him up if he was to be boiled alive! Murderer! Murderer! Down with him!

Charley flings himself at Sikes and brings him crashing to the floor.

Charley   Murderer! Help! Help!

Sikes gets the better of him and has his hands on his throat. Suddenly Dodger pulls Sikes back.

Dodger   Bill! Listen!

Noises on the stairs.

They're coming!

From outside.

Policeman   Open the door, in the King's name!

Charley   He's here! He's here! Break down the door!

Policeman   Open up!

Charley   Break it down! They'll never open it!

Dodger   Charley!

Sikes   Give me a rope! I'm going over the roofs! Give me a rope or I'll murder two more!

Dodger throws him a rope. Sikes rushes out. Crash as the door is broken down.

Policeman   Don't move, you two!

Charley   He's gone up the back way! He's going over the roofs!

Policeman   Hold these two! And follow me!

1st Pursuer   We've got him now!

Brownlow   I will give fifty pounds to the man who takes him alive!

2nd Pursuer   Come on! Hang him! Hang him!

Policeman   Some of you watch the front!

Music. Some race after Sikes, some back through the door, dragging Dodger and Charley with them. Sikes dashes up a flight of stairs.

Sikes   I'll cheat them yet!

He stops dead. The ghost of Nancy looms before him.

Nancy! No, Nancy, let me be!

Oliver There he goes!

Sikes Do your worst! I'll cheat you yet!

He flees up the stairs.

Policeman Where is he?

Oliver Up there! Look!

2nd Pursuer What's he doing?

Oliver He's heading over the roofs.

Charley He's got a rope. He's going to let himself down into the ditch.

Policeman Stop or I'll fire!

Dodger makes a dash for it.

Hey! Stop him!

3rd Pursuer Hold the boy!

Sikes Nancy!

There is a sudden scream from above and a body falls, dangling by its neck from a rope. Music and blackout.

Scene Thirty-Four

Lights up on the condemned cell. Fagin alone. A bell is tolling ten. There is sporadic hammering outside. As the tolling ends Brownlow and Oliver appear outside the cell with a Jailer.

Jailer This is it. Here – the young gentleman's not going in, is he, sir? It's not a sight for children.

Brownlow Indeed it isn't. But he's very much involved in my business with this man.

Noise of hammering.

What's that?

Jailer   They're preparing the gallows. This is the way he'll go in the morning. That's the door he'll go out at to his hanging.

They enter the cell.

Fagin   Good boy, Charley – well done. Oliver too – ha! ha! ha! Oliver too – quite the gentleman now – quite the – take the boy away to bed.

Jailer   (*to Oliver*) Don't be alarmed.

Fagin   Take him away to bed. Do you hear me? He has been the – somehow the cause of all this. No. Monks. Monks's throat, Bill. Never mind Nancy. Monks's throat as deep as you can cut. Saw his head off!

Jailer   Fagin.

Fagin   That's me. An old man, my lord, a very old, old man!

Noise of hammering.

Jailer   Here's someone wants to see you, to ask some questions, I suppose. Fagin, Fagin, are you a man?

Fagin   I shan't be one much longer. Strike them all dead! What right have they to butcher me?

He suddenly takes notice of Brownlow and Oliver.

What do they want here?

Jailer   Steady! Now, sir, tell him what you want. Quick, please – he's growing worse as the time gets on.

Jailer goes out. Noise of hammering.

Brownlow   You have some papers, which were placed in your hands, for safe keeping, by a man called Monks.

Fagin   Papers? What papers?

Brownlow   You know very well. It's a will. A will bequeathing to Oliver here all his father's fortune – money which would otherwise go to his half-brother,

	Monks, if Oliver died…or if Oliver ever fell foul of the law. You know that, don't you? That's why Monks wanted you to make Oliver a thief, isn't it? That's why Monks was so desperate to destroy the locket – the only proof of Oliver's identity. You know all this. So where are those papers?
Fagin	Why should *you* care? What will *you* gain? Tell me that.
Brownlow	Come on.
Fagin	No. Tell me! Watch him, Oliver! He'll cheat you – he'll turn the money to his own account – they're all the same! Why should he work so hard in your behalf?
Brownlow	I care because he's my grandson!

Silence. Fagin and Oliver are both astonished.

	I'd have told you in a happier place than this, Oliver, but it's true! You remember the picture that you loved so much? The picture of the lady, who looked so much like you? That sweet young woman was your mother – and my daughter! So now you know, Fagin. Now where are those papers for my grandson?
Fagin	It's all a lie! I haven't one! Not one!
Brownlow	For the love of God, don't say that now, upon the very verge of death! Tell me where they are. You know that Sikes is dead, your boys will be transported, that Monks has confessed – there is no hope of further gain. Where are those papers?
Fagin	Oliver, here, here. Let me whisper to you.

Oliver turns to Brownlow.

Oliver	I'm not afraid.
Fagin	The papers are in a canvas bag, in a hole a little way up the chimney in the top front room. I want to talk to you, Oliver.
Oliver	All right. All right. Let me say a prayer. Say just one, on your knees with me, and we'll talk till morning.
Fagin	Escape, Oliver! You can help me escape! I'll slip

away, and you can say I've gone to sleep. They'll believe *you*. You can get me out if you hide me. Easy as pie. Look, look! Let's go! Now! Now!

Oliver   Oh God forgive him!

Fagin   Through the door. Through the door. If I shake as we pass the gallows don't mind me – just hurry on. Now! Now! Now!

The Jailer re-enters.

Jailer   Have you nothing else to ask him, sir?

Brownlow   No. If I thought we could recall him to his senses –

Jailer   Nothing will do that, sir. You'd better leave him.

Brownlow   Very well. Oliver.

Brownlow and Oliver start to go.

Fagin   Don't leave me! Don't leave me with these butchers!

Brownlow   He told you where the papers are?

Oliver   Yes, sir.

Brownlow   Thank God! You're a rich young man, Oliver!

Oliver   Yes, sir.

Brownlow   Come on.

Noise of hammering.

Fagin   Don't leave me, Oliver! You know what they're going to do to Fagin! Don't leave me here!

But they've gone. Two Workmen appear with sledgehammers. The Jailer meets them outside the cell.

Jailer   All finished?

Workman   Ay. It's ready.

They go. Music. The lights slowly fade to black with Fagin slumped in the cell.

Alternative Scene Twenty-Seven
(if doubling **Grimwig** and **Monks**)

Grimwig's house.

Brownlow Bring the boy into the back room! There are two constables coming up the drive! We must sort this out before we see the police!

Rose hurries in with Oliver.

Now, Oliver, you say they forced you to it?

Oliver Yes, sir, upon my word. Mr Sikes dragged me here in the dead of night, and I didn't know what it was for until they – they drew out their masks and pistols, sir. Then they pushed me through the – through the –

Brownlow The trap-door.

Oliver Yes. And I remember nothing more. And now I – please, I –

Brownlow Oh, poor boy! Poor boy! Rose, I'm taking him home with me.

Rose pulls Brownlow aside.

Rose But Mr Brownlow, you can't! Father says he's a liar and a thief, and he's fooled you once already.

Brownlow And I'll be fooled again! If it means the boy can be safe and well I'll be fooled again! If the police arrest him he'll be dead within a week.

Ring of the doorbell.

Rose They're here!

Brownlow Rose, don't let Grimwig tell the police about Oliver! Tell him to give them a full report about the burglary, but to say nothing about the boy.

Rose But Mr Brownlow –

Brownlow He's ill, Rose! And I believe him – twice, yes, I believe him! I'm taking Oliver home to Pentonville, and your father will have to eat his head!

QUESTIONS AND EXPLORATIONS

1 Keeping Track

Scene One

1 What is the Surgeon's attitude to the woman he is helping to give birth?

2 What is your first impression of Oliver's start in life?

Scenes Two and Three

1 How do you react to Mr Bumble's description of choosing children's names?

2 Why do you think the dishes are part of the stage props?

3 Why are the Master, Mr Bumble and the Board Members so shocked at Oliver's question?

Scenes Four and Five

1 Mr Sowerberry and Mr Bumble discuss coffins. What do you find out about coffin sizes and costs?

2 Why does the man in the hovel say 'They killed her!'? Whom is he accusing and do you think he is right?

3 The old Woman Pauper, mother of the dead girl, says '...it's as good as a play!' Why do you think she says this?

Scene Six

1 What drives Oliver to pounce on Noah?

2 Noah laughs at his own joke: 'All his relations let him have his own way pretty well, eh, Charlotte?' Why is this particularly cruel?

3   How does Charlotte treat Noah?

4   How do his enemies describe Oliver to Mr Bumble? Do you think this is accurate?

Scenes Seven

1   The Dodger says, about Oliver, '...he ain't twigged yet!' meaning that Oliver hasn't understood the double meanings in his words. Find some more words the Dodger uses that have these double meanings. What are the two (or more) meanings of the words?

2   Who is the 'respectable old gentleman' to whom the Dodger refers?

3   Why does the Dodger look after Oliver so well?

Scenes Eight and Nine

1   What evidence can you find in these scenes that Fagin's gang are criminals? Does Oliver understand the meaning of what he sees and hears in Fagin's den? Give reasons for your answer.

2   What is your impression of the hideout and its residents?

3   Oliver is 'jolly green', as Charley Bates says in Scene 9. Do you think the treatment of Oliver in this scene is comic or tragic? Why do you think so?

Scenes Ten and Eleven

1   How would you describe Oliver's behaviour in Scene 10?

2   How many different thefts are mentioned in Scene 10? When you have read both scenes, do you find the number is the same?

3 What impression of the law do you get from observing Mr Fang? Give examples of his actions and what you think of them.

Scene Twelve

1 How have Charley and the Dodger made Oliver look guilty?

2 Why is Fagin, and then Bill Sikes too, worried about Oliver being in the hands of the police?

3 What do they want Nancy to do? Why do they think she is most suited to the job?

4 Look at Nancy's behaviour towards Bill. How is it different from the way Charlotte treats Noah in Scene 6?

Scene Thirteen

1 How is Oliver's treatment in this scene different from all that has happened to him until now?

2 Mr Brownlow is surprised by Oliver's likeness to the portrait. Look back to Scene 11 and find the words that show he had already noticed a resemblance. What do you think this might suggest about Oliver's relatives?

Scenes Fourteen and Fifteen

1 Nancy is not acting as herself. What role does she play here?

2 Why do you think Scene 14 was put between the scenes on either side?

3 How are Mr Brownlow's and Mr Grimwig's opinions of Oliver different?

Scene Sixteen

1　Read this scene *before* looking at the next two. Try to predict what will happen to Oliver in these scenes.

Scenes Seventeen and Eighteen

1　How near to your prediction are the events in these scenes?

2　How do Nancy and Sikes fool the woman who questions them? Look back at question 1 from Scene 14. Has Nancy changed or developed her role?

3　How do you react to Oliver being captured?

Scene Nineteen

1　There is no dialogue in this scene. Why is the scene here?

Scene Twenty

1　Nigel Bryant has made the interval follow this scene. Why has he chosen this particular place for the interval?

Scenes Twenty-One, Twenty-Two and Twenty-Three

1　Mr Bumble asks Mrs Mann, 'Are *you* hard-hearted, Mrs Mann?' Is she? Explain how you think she behaves (a) towards Mr Bumble and (b) towards the paupers.

2　Nancy tells Oliver that Bill is planning to use him 'For no good, then.' What do you think he will use him for?

Scenes Twenty-Four and Twenty-Five

1　How does the plan go wrong?

Scene Twenty-Six

1 Fagin tells Nancy that he '...with six words can strangle Sikes as surely as if I had his bull's head between my fingers now.' What does he mean?

2 What has Nancy been doing while Fagin and Monks have been talking?

Scene Twenty-Seven (or Alternative Scene Twenty-Seven at the end of the play)

1 It is a coincidence that Mr Brownlow happens to be involved again when Oliver is badly hurt. What do you think of the use of coincidence to make the plot work? (It is used by Dickens in the original novel as well as in Nigel Bryant's play.)

Scenes Twenty-Eight and Twenty-Nine

1 What is the coincidence to which Monks refers?

2 Mrs Mann and Mr Bumble are partners in the plot against Oliver. Which one is cleverer about money?

Scenes Thirty, Thirty-One and Thirty-Two

1 Think about what Nancy does and says in these scenes. Does she betray Sikes?

2 What are your feelings about the murder of Nancy?

Scenes Thirty-Three and Thirty-Four

1 How does Sikes' escape plan go wrong?

2 Is the end of Scene 34 a sad or a happy ending? Say why you give that answer.

2 Explorations

A Novel into Play

1 Read the following extract from Dickens' novel. (Some of Dickens' vocabulary is explained on page 98.)

The room in which the boys were fed was a large stone hall, with a copper at one end: out of which the master, dressed in an apron for the purpose, and assisted by one or two women, ladled the gruel at meal-times. Of this festive composition each boy had one porringer, and no more – except on occasions of great public rejoicing, when he had two ounces and a quarter of bread besides. The bowls never wanted washing. The boys polished them with their spoons till they shone again; and when they had performed this operation (which never took very long, the spoons being nearly as large as the bowls), they would sit staring at the copper, with such eager eyes, as if they could have devoured the very bricks of which it was composed; employing themselves, meanwhile, in sucking their fingers most assiduously, with the view of catching up any stray splashes of gruel that might have been cast thereon. Boys have generally excellent appetites. Oliver Twist and his companions suffered the tortures of slow starvation for three months: at last they got so voracious and wild with hunger, that one boy, who was tall for his age, and hadn't been used to that sort of thing (for his father had kept a small cook-shop), hinted darkly to his companions, that unless he had another basin of gruel *per diem*, he was afraid he might some night happen to eat the boy who slept next him, who happened to be a weakly youth of tender age. He had a wild, hungry eye; and they implicitly believed him. A council was held; lots were cast who should walk up to the master after supper that evening, and ask for more; and it fell to Oliver Twist.

The evening arrived; the boys took their places. The master, in his cook's uniform, stationed himself at the copper; his pauper assistants ranged themselves behind him; the gruel was served out; and a long grace was said over the short commons. The gruel disappeared; the boys whispered each other, and winked at Oliver; while his next neighbour nudged him. Child as he was, he was desperate with hunger, and reckless with misery. He rose from the table; and advancing to the master, basin and spoon in hand, said, somewhat alarmed at his own temerity –

"Please, sir, I want some more."

The master was a fat, healthy man; but he turned very pale. He gazed in stupefied astonishment on the small rebel for some seconds, and then clung for support to the copper. The assistants were paralysed with wonder; the boys with fear.

"What!" said the master at length, in a faint voice.

"Please, sir," replied Oliver, "I want some more."

The master aimed a blow at Oliver's head with the ladle, pinioned him in his arms, and shrieked aloud for the beadle.

The Board were sitting in solemn conclave, when Mr. Bumble rushed into the room in great excitement, and addressing the gentleman in the high chair, said –

"Mr. Limbkins, I beg your pardon, sir! Oliver Twist has asked for more!"

There was a general start. Horror was depicted on every countenance.

"For *more!*" said Mr. Limbkins. "Compose yourself, Mr. Bumble, and answer me distinctly. Do I understand that he asked for more, after he had eaten the supper allotted by the dietary?"

"He did, sir," replied Bumble.

"That boy will be hung," said the gentleman in the white waistcoat. "I know that boy will be hung."

Nobody controverted the prophetic gentleman's opinion. An animated discussion took place. Oliver was ordered into instant confinement; and a bill was next morning pasted on the outside of the gate, offering a reward of five pounds to anybody who would take Oliver Twist off the hands of the parish. In other words, five pounds and Oliver Twist were offered to any man or woman who wanted an apprentice to any trade, business, or calling.

"I never was more convinced of anything in my life," said the gentleman in the white waistcoat, as he knocked at the gate and read the bill next morning: "I never was more convinced of anything in my life, than I am that that boy will come to be hung."

copper	container made of copper, set in bricks, for cooking
porringer	small dish for soup or porridge
per diem	daily
commons	food put out on a central table
temerity	recklessness
conclave	private meeting

2   Now re-read Scene 3 from Nigel Bryant's adaptation of the novel, from *Exit Bumble* to the end of this famous scene. In his novel Dickens uses narrative and description to tell us about places and people. The play version must put this into stage directions, dialogue or simply leave it out. In these next activities, you will be comparing the two versions to see how they are different.

3   In Dickens' version, what are we told about the canteen and how the boys eat?

4   Look at the two versions and find the part where the boys plan to send Oliver to ask for more. How does Dickens *tell* you and how does Bryant *show* you? Is the plan the same in each? What extra details are there in one or the other?

5   Are Oliver's words the same in each?

6   Dickens has a gentleman in a white waistcoat. Who does Bryant use instead? Are their words the same?

7   Dickens tells us what the master looks like and how he is dressed. What sort of costume would suit him? If you were the director, how would you ask him to stand, speak and move?

8   Dickens tells us the master 'served out' the gruel. What word does Bryant use and why?

9   This scene is the most famous in the novel. It gives a

very strong visual impression, just as the play does. In groups, produce a freeze-frame (tableau) for each of the following 'pictures' in the scene:

from Dickens

a) the boys looking forward to their meal
b) the master clinging onto the copper, with everyone looking on
c) Mr Bumble dragging Oliver into the meeting of the Board

from Bryant

d) several boys telling Oliver about the workhouse rules
e) Oliver picking the short straw
f) Oliver asking for more

B   Staging the Play

Dickens considered becoming an actor himself and was involved in the world of the theatre all his life. Below is an artist's impression of a nineteenth-century theatre audience.

The next two illustrations from an early edition of the novel show how Oliver, Bill Sikes and Fagin were presented at Her Majesty's Theatre in London in the late nineteenth century. The actor-manager Beerbohm Tree played Fagin, and Oliver was played by Mrs Keeley.

1 You can see from the old photographs how these characters were costumed. Design costumes you think would suit the Artful Dodger and Mr Bumble.

2 Re-read Scene 8, taking note of what you find out about Fagin's hideout. Read also what Nigel Bryant says in his introduction on the staging of the play at the Victoria Theatre. Now draw a set from this scene and label the furniture to go into it. What props (smaller articles) might be needed?

C   Sentimentality and Melodrama (see Glossary)

In Dickens' day, many people enjoyed reading sentimental descriptions of perfectly-good children, like Oliver, or Tiny Tim in *A Christmas Carol*. Perhaps this was because they wanted children to be like them. Today, we may find such characters dull and hard to like. People also enjoyed reading about wicked characters such as Bill Sikes and Fagin who are, so evil that their behaviour is melodramatic or sensational. You may feel such exaggerated goodness or wickedness is unrealistic, or it may add to your enjoyment of the characters' behaviour.

1   In groups, read aloud Scene 13, as it was intended to be read. You could act it too. Make Oliver behave perfectly. Then, keeping everyone else the same, change Oliver to a short-tempered, obnoxious brat. Discuss this first, and then try acting it out. Don't write any script. Improvise! The group will need to respond to the new-style Oliver in a new way.

2   In groups, read aloud Scene 30, as it was intended to be read, as far as the point where Sikes goes to sleep. Make Sikes as horrible as he should be. Then, keeping everyone else the same, change Sikes to a reasonable person, thankful for Nancy's care. Improvise a new scene. As with the activity above, talk about how to do this before you act it. Don't write a new script.

3   Decide which version of each scene is more realistic.

D   Music and Sound Effects

1   Imagine you are producing a radio reading of the script. In pairs, or in groups, choose or try to create suitable music and sound effects to introduce the following scenes: 5, 8, 17, 34.

2   You might want additional music or sound effects during
    the scenes too. Record your rehearsed reading of one of
    these scenes with accompanying music and sound
    effects.

E   Film Versions

The Time Out Film Guide lists reviews of films.

1   Read the Key to the reviews and the three reviews which
    follow.

Key to the reviews

Titles are filed in directory order (ignoring word divisions). Thus:
Dance of the Vampires/Dancers/Dance with a Stranger.

Following the title(s), each entry lists (in parentheses) the name of
the director, the date of the film, and the country of origin; the
leading members of the cast; the running time; the annotation 'b/w'
if the film is in black-and-white, 'b/w & col' if it has one or more
sequences in colour. No annotation after the running time means
the film is in colour. If the film is available on video the details
follow.

The **date given** is normally the registration date, not the release
date (which may or may not be the same, depending on whether
release of a film was delayed). The **country of origin** indicates
where the film was financed, not where it was made. The **running
time** given is that of the longest known version (many release prints
are, of course, cut for one reason or another). Since many films are
circulated in different versions in different countries, recorded
running times are at best approximate.

Oliver!

(Carol Reed, 1968, GB) Ron Moody, Shani Wallis, Oliver Reed, Harry
Secombe, Hugh Griffith, Jack Wild, Clive Moss, Mark Lester, Peggy Mount,
Leonard Rossiter.
146 min. U. Video: Prestwich Operations.
£9.99 **VHS** CVT20048.
From *The Third Man* to *Oliver!* is a pretty vertiginous collapse, even for
twenty years in the British film industry. Reed is craftsman enough to make

an efficient family entertainment out of Lionel Bart's musical, but not artist enough to put back any of Dickens' teeth which Bart had so assiduously drawn.

Oliver Twist

(David Lean, 1948, GB) John Howard Davies, Alec Guinness, Robert Newton, Kay Walsh, Francis L. Sullivan, Henry Stephenson, Mary Clare, Anthony Newley, Kathleen Harrison, Diana Dors.
116 min. b/w.
Lean's second Dickens adaptation, perhaps marginally less beguiling than *Great Expectations*, but still a moving and enjoyable account of Dickens' masterpiece, which gets off to a memorable start with Oliver's pregnant mother battling through the storm to reach the safety of the workhouse. The film tellingly recreates the horrors of Victorian slum life (the attractive if artificial sets atmospherically lit and shot by Guy Green), and is particularly noteworthy for Guinness' striking Fagin.

Oliver Twist

(Clive Donner, 1982, GB) George C Scott, Tim Curry, Michael Hordern, Timothy West, Eileen Atkins, Cherie Lunghi, Oliver Cotton, Richard Charles, Martin Tempest.
102 min. PG Video: Channel 5. £9.99 **VHS** CFV00602.
Yet another helping of *Oliver Twist*, all too clearly showing its TV origins? What the Dickens could it possibly have to offer that Lean's 1948 version or Reed's all-singing, all-dancing *Oliver!* haven't already given us? Not a lot, unless it's a timely illustration of the Return to Victorian Values that everyone's going on about. (Gin at a penny a pint? We should be so lucky.) George C Scott, as Fagin, gives an interesting new transatlantic flavour to the proceedings, but otherwise fails to generate anything other than total disbelief. A dollop of dirt on the face of some precocious brat does not make for a really convincing waif: and an *Oliver Twist* that leaves one sympathising with Bill Sikes must surely have taken a wrong turning somewhere.

2   Now complete the Film Quiz below. You can check your answers against the list which follows the Glossary.

Film Quiz

a) Which is the earliest version?

b) Who directed the most recent one?

c) How many are black and white?

d) Which is the film of the musical?

e) Which director's film has a favourable review?

f) Who played Fagin in the latest film?

g) Who played him in 1948?

h) How many versions are now available on video?

i) Which is the longest film?

j) Which director made an earlier Dickens film?

F Types of Language

Nigel Bryant has put much of the original dialogue into his characters' mouths. (The Glossary at the back of the book can help you with some words you may not know.) Although all of it is English, it is not all the same kind of English. The language changes to reflect the character using it: Mr Brownlow speaks politely and doesn't use slang, Mr Bumble makes mistakes when he talks ('supernatural exertions', Scene 2, 'obstinater young rascal', Scene 28) and Fagin and the slum-dwellers speak a kind of slang or jargon which shows their criminal background.

1   In pairs, write down your ideas about:

   a) why Oliver, despite his workhouse life, always speaks pleasantly and politely

   b) why Mr Bumble's English has mistakes in it

   c) why the Dodger's language is full of double meanings

   d) why Bill Sikes, rather than anyone else, is racist when he talks to Fagin

   e) why the criminals sometimes suddenly speak in an educated way: Dodger, for example, says 'I have a violent antipathy to police stations' (Scene 12) and Nancy says 'to make me suffer such distress on your account!' (Scene 18)

G   Partners in Crime

1   Work with another person using the character list at the start of the play.

   a) Which six characters work together as male/female pairs to cause Oliver trouble?

   b) Arrange them in pairs, putting the female character first if she is the stronger partner, the male if he is the stronger one. What do you discover?

   c) List all six in order of wickedness, with the most evil first.

   d) How many of them are punished in the play? Find out what happens to Dodger by reading Chapter 43 of the novel.

   e) Do you have sympathy with any of them? Discuss your opinions with each other.

   f) Do any of them have exaggerated or absurd names? Do any of the 'good' characters have names of this sort given to them? Why do you think Dickens chose these names?

GLOSSARY

A number of the words and phrases in this glossary are no longer in use. Others are part of the slang that Dickens used to suggest the way Fagin's criminals might have spoken.

	Page	
ague	73	shivering fever
bath chair	36	invalid chair, first used in the town of Bath
beadle	3	a parish officer
Bedlam	12	a hospital for mentally-ill people (first called St Mary of Bethlehem, shortened to Bedlam); without capital, used today to mean noisy chaos
Botany Bay	18	place in Australia to which British convicts were transported; Dodger risks being sent there
Bridewell Prison	15	a jail where unmarried mothers were sent
cockalorum	32	conceited little person; a children's jumping game
covey or *cove*	18	fellow or mate
crack	60	attempted robbery
cravat	12	a man's neckcloth
destitute	vii	in absolute poverty
dietary	9	parish rules controlling the food eaten by workhouse inmates

drab	62	slut
fence	33	someone who receives stolen goods
fogle	27	silk handkerchief
Gadso!	10	short for 'Gadsooks!', an outdated exclamation
gruel	2	watery oatmeal porridge
hand was not in	63	hadn't got the knack
heavy swell cut	44	stylish
jargon	104	kind of slang used by a particular group employed in the same activity
laudanum	72	sleeping drug
lush	19	drink
mealy	40	powdery-white
melodrama	101	over-sensational drama, using horror and with a sickly-sweet ending; sometimes accompanied by music
oakum	6	old rope that could be picked apart for filling gaps between the boards of a ship; a job for prisoners
pauper	11	a person in absolute poverty, usually living in a workhouse
peached	34	betrayed
plant	26	good target for pickpocketing
Plummy and slam!	20	password to enter Fagin's den
privy	7	toilet
sentimentality	101	overflowing emotion, too much sweetness and charm

swag	51	stolen goods
swipes	19	spoilt beer
tinkler	59	doorbell
togs	44	clothes
Toor rul lol, etc.	32	phrases from popular songs of the day
traps	33	thief-catchers
treadmill	19	cylinder made to turn by prisoners treading attached boards; used as a punishment

Answers to Film Quiz

a) 1948
b) Clive Donner
c) One
d) *Oliver!*
e) David Lean
f) George C. Scott
g) Alec Guinness
h) 2
i) *Oliver!*
j) David Lean